Beyond Bev ___ge

Beyond Beveridge

*Restoring the contributory principle
to retirement pensions
and welfare benefits*

Peter Saunders

CIVITAS
INSTITUTE FOR THE STUDY
OF CIVIL SOCIETY · LONDON

First Published November 2013

© Civitas 2013
55 Tufton Street
London SW1P 3QL

email: books@civitas.org.uk

ISBN 978-1-906837-57-0

Independence: Civitas: Institute for the Study of Civil Society is a
registered educational charity (No. 1085494) and a company limited by
guarantee (No. 04023541). Civitas is financed from a variety of private
sources to avoid over-reliance on any single or small group of donors.

All publications are independently refereed. All the Institute's
publications seek to further its objective of promoting the advancement
of learning. The views expressed are those of the authors, not of the
Institute.

Designed and typeset by
Richard Kelly

Printed in Great Britain by
Berforts Group Ltd
Stevenage SG1 2BH

Contents

Acknowledgements

Thanks to Catherine Hakim for her thorough and very helpful comments on an earlier draft, and to John Hills for guidance on interpreting his lifetime tax/welfare model. Thanks also to David Green and Civitas for their patient support, to Robert Whelan for his painstaking editing, and to Greg Lindsay and the Centre for Independent Studies for permission to re-use some material in Part I that originally appeared in my 2013 CIS Occasional Paper *Remoralising the Welfare State*.

Author

Peter Saunders is a Professorial Fellow of Civitas, and author of *Social Mobility Myths* and *The Rise of the Equalities Industry*, published by Civitas in 2010 and 2011 respectively. Until 1999, he was Professor of Sociology at the University of Sussex, where he is still Professor Emeritus, and he has held visiting academic posts at universities in Australia, Germany, New Zealand and the United States. After 1999, he worked as Research Manager at the Australian Institute of Family Studies, and as Social Research Director at the Centre for Independent Studies in Sydney, where he remains a Distinguished Fellow. In 2008 he returned to the UK where he is an independent writer and consultant. In addition to his work for Civitas, his publications include *A Nation of Home Owners; Capitalism—A Social Audit; Social Theory and the Urban Question; Introduction to British Politics; Privatisation and Popular Capitalism, Australia's welfare habit and how to kick it* and, most recently, *When Prophecy Fails*. More details of his work can be found at www.petersaunders.org.uk.

Executive Summary

This report reviews Britain's National Insurance system and proposes that it be replaced by compulsory 'personal welfare accounts', developed from the new workplace pensions scheme. A move to personal accounts would overcome many of the weaknesses and problems in the current NI system while strengthening the vital 'contributory principle' at its core. It would reduce pressure on the public finances as well as delivering an effective system of social security which is responsive to people's needs and widely regarded as fair by the public.

◆ Britain's National Insurance system was established by William Beveridge on the principle that everyone who is capable of working should contribute from their earnings to a fund which would pay for their retirement and tide them over during periods of sickness or unemployment during their working lives. Taxpayer-funded welfare benefits were to be a last resort.

◆ This contributory principle is widely supported by the British public because it taps into an instinctive sense of fairness which we all share. While most of us believe people who are in need of help should be assisted in some way (the need principle), we also believe that people who take should, if possible, give something in return (the fairness, or proportionality, principle). Both of these principles have been shown to be instinctive, having evolved over many years of human and social development.

◆ Over the last 70 years, the contributory principle at the heart of Beveridge's National Insurance system has been eroded, and taxpayer-funded hand-outs have increasingly replaced contributions-based benefits. As a result, our belief in the fairness of the welfare system has ebbed away. Increasingly, the welfare state has concerned itself simply with the relief of need, and has paid less and less regard to the equally important principle of fair treatment. The system may still be compassionate, but it is no longer seen as fair.

◆ Today, people are treated as if they have paid contributions when they haven't, and claimants with no contributions record get treated much the same as those who have being paying contributions all their lives. The new state pension will be worth only £1.30 per week more for someone with 35 years of NI contributions than someone with no contributions can receive in Pension Credit. Unemployment and sickness payments to those with full contributions records are no higher than for those without. Britain is almost alone in Europe in paying unemployed people with weak or non-existent employment records the same as those with a long history of employment.

◆ As the boundary between contributory and non-contributory benefits has become blurred, critics have started calling for National Insurance to be wound up altogether. They point out that National Insurance bears little resemblance anymore to 'insurance' and has effectively become just another tax on incomes, albeit a very opaque one. Many of us are unaware how much NI we are paying (directly, through our own contributions, and indirectly, through those paid on our behalf by our employers). Nor do we understand what our contributions are buying (when asked about this, more people mention the NHS than pensions, yet the NHS is mainly funded out of general taxation). The case for reform is compelling.

◆ Scrapping National Insurance would undermine the case for a universal state retirement pension. For as long as the state pension is based on contributions, it should not be means-tested, for contributions buy entitlement. But if it begins to be financed out of general tax revenues, the argument for means-testing becomes stronger, for taxpayers should not have to fund welfare payments for people who do not need them.

◆ The cost of state pensions is forecast to rise from £84bn to £250bn over the next 40 years. The Organisation for Economic Co-operation and Development recently warned the UK government that if it fails to cut this spiralling cost, both the state pension and NHS could collapse. Means-testing the state pension could be part of the answer, saving an estimated £40 billion each year when fully implemented.

◆ Means-testing the state pension would require enrolment in the new work-based pensions scheme to be made compulsory for all workers (at present, it is possible to opt out). This would be necessary to guard against moral hazard problems (people deliberately failing to save to make themselves eligible for a means-tested state pension). Making retirement saving compulsory could begin to rescue and strengthen Beveridge's contributory principle, even as National Insurance is abolished.

◆ The welfare state already operates like a system of compulsory saving. It not only redistributes resources from rich to poor; it also spreads people's incomes more evenly over their own lifetimes. Three-quarters of government spending on the welfare state involves income smoothing (returning money to people at one time in their lives after taking it off them at another), rather than redistribution. Even the lowest 10 per cent of lifetime earners pay in taxes for nearly half of all the welfare benefits and services they receive during their lives. Most of us should therefore be able to afford to save and insure more in our accounts if the government reduced the amount it takes to spend on our behalf.

◆ The problem with Beveridge's National Insurance system was not that it required people to fund their own benefits, but that it gave them no control over what happened to their contributions. Moving to a system of personal welfare accounts would give people more control over their own savings. It would be more efficient than having the government doing it for us, it would strengthen work and savings incentives, and it would promote a stronger sense of personal and civic responsibility.

◆ Income can be spread over a lifetime by saving (useful for predictable events like retirement), insurance (needed to cover high-cost but unpredictable events like long-term disability) and loans (which can be used to pay in advance for things like higher education where the cost can be recouped from later earnings). Personal welfare accounts should be used in all three ways.

◆ Like existing workplace pensions, their core function should be to save for retirement. With the abolition of National Insurance, they should also be used to cover non-catastrophic risks like short-term unemployment and sickness, and short periods of parental leave. Requiring people to fund absences from work from their own savings, rather than drawing on taxpayer-funded benefits, will create a disincentive to claim unless the condition is genuine.

◆ Under certain circumstances, people should be allowed to borrow against their accounts to help fund short periods of unemployment, as well as paying higher education fees from them. Accounts should also be used to insure against future nursing home fees, and could help reduce cost pressures on the NHS if patients drew on them to pay a 'deductible' to help with the cost of medical treatment, or to make a contribution towards ancillary items like hospital 'hotel' charges.

The report makes eight specific policy recommendations:

1. Wind up the National Insurance system:
The employee 12 per cent contribution should be added to the basic income tax rate making a new basic rate of 32 per cent (with appropriate adjustments for older workers, the self-employed and people receiving income from savings and pensions). The higher tax rate should rise to 42 per cent to take account of the two per cent NIC levied on earnings above the upper earnings limit. The 13.8 per cent employers' NICs should become a Payroll Tax.

2. Establish entitlement to the new state pension through residency
Scrapping NICs means new eligibility rules are needed for the state pension. Eligibility should depend on 10+ years of residency in this country. Pension Credit should be abolished.

3. Phase in a state pension means-test for new retirees
Over the next 40 years, if NICs are abolished now, the contributory component of people's state pensions will gradually get smaller, and the taxpayer-funded component will get larger, until eventually the whole of every state pension claim will be funded out of tax revenues. The tax-funded component of state pensions should be means-tested.

4. Freeze current National Insurance entitlements and recognise them as government debt
Entitlements based on contributions up to the time National Insurance is scrapped should be honoured by freezing people's NIC records, indexing their existing entitlement to take account of inflation, and paying this amount as a weekly or monthly pension from when they retire. The future cost of these payments (currently estimated at £3.8 trillion) should be explicitly acknowledged as part of total public sector borrowing.

5: Make membership of workplace pension schemes compulsory
The right of workers to opt out of workplace pensions should be ended. With a means-tested state pension, saving in private retirement accounts has to be made compulsory to minimise moral hazard.

6. Boost personal retirement savings accounts
Minimum contributions into the new workplace pensions schemes add up to 11 per cent of salary (combining the employee's and employer's contribution, and adding the value of government tax relief). This is too low to guarantee self-reliance in retirement. Contributions should be boosted by reducing the government's tax-take from employees and employers. In particular, savings accruing from means-testing the state pension should be used to reduce the

employer Payroll Tax from 13.8 per cent to 12 per cent (switching the 1.8 per cent reduction into an enhanced employer contribution to workplace pensions), and the basic rate of income tax for employees from 32 per cent to 30 per cent (switching the 2 per cent reduction into an enhanced employee contribution to the workplace pension). This would take the minimum total contribution into workplace pensions to almost 15 per cent. Proceeds from privatisation of Royal Mail and the state-owned bank assets should also be used to boost workers' pension accounts.

7. Gradually extend the permitted uses of workplace pension funds to develop them into personal welfare accounts
Contributory unemployment and sickness benefits should be scrapped two years after NICs are ended (all claimants would then get the non-contributory Universal Credit). At the same time, people should be allowed to use their personal welfare accounts (or borrow against them) to provide a benefits-level income for the first 6 months out of work, during which time there should be no conditions applied to them. Existing and future student loans should be integrated into personal welfare accounts and, over time, accounts should be further extended to cover periods of parental leave to care for children and basic insurance against old-age care costs.

8. Apply activity conditions to receipt of working-age benefits
Unconditional support for people who cannot be expected to work (severely disabled people and single parents with infant children under one year) should continue, but for those who are capable of working full- or part-time, and who cannot support themselves from their own personal welfare accounts, fairness requires that appropriate work-based activity conditions should be attached to receipt of state benefits. No activity conditions should be attached

to jobless people drawing on their own personal welfare accounts.

INTRODUCTION

Britain's system of National Insurance was a grand project designed for a time that has passed. Many experts now believe it has outlived its usefulness. The system has been subject to so much change and tinkering over the last seventy years that it is now almost unrecognisable from the one we started out with after World War II. It is no longer fit for purpose, which is why many observers think the most sensible option is to scrap it altogether.

But there is something uniquely important about Britain's National Insurance system which must not be lost. It is the principle that people establish a right to benefits by making regular contributions into a fund throughout their working lives.

When William Beveridge first outlined his plans for the new National Insurance system in the 1940s, he emphasised that everyone who is capable of doing so should make provision for their long-term needs by contributing to a fund. This 'contributory principle' was based on the simple idea that if you expect to be supported later on, you should be required to pay something now, while you can. This foundation principle of our National Insurance system is as valid and compelling today as it was seventy years ago. Unfortunately, our National Insurance system nowadays has ceased to take it seriously.

National Insurance is in a sorry state. Its design no longer fits current needs and it requires a radical re-think. But to allow the whole thing to collapse without rescuing and restoring the contributory principle at its heart would be a major mistake for which future generations would rightly chide us.

Most of the critics are economists. It has been said that economists know the price of everything and the value of nothing, which is unfair, for market prices tell us a lot about what people really value. But by looking at *everything* in terms of costs and benefits, pounds and pence, economists do sometimes focus on efficiency problems at the expense of social and moral questions which are equally important.

It is mainly on grounds of efficiency that economists have looked at our National Insurance system and concluded that it is beyond repair. They deplore the fact that it delivers pensions and benefits to people who may not need the money. Given that we want state welfare to help those in most need, they say, why don't we target scarce funds on those who really need help, rather than spraying money around to anyone who happens to have paid National Insurance contributions (NICs)?

They also worry about the overhead costs of the system. They point to the administrative burden on employers who have to calculate and collect income tax deductions according to one set of rules, and then have to calculate and collect National Insurance deductions according to another. Wouldn't it be easier, say the economists, to fold NICs into the income tax system so deductions have only to be calculated once?

And they criticise the opaqueness of the present system. They point to the widespread public misunderstanding about what National Insurance is funding (many people wrongly believe that it pays for the National Health Service, for example). They highlight public ignorance about how it works (many people assume that their contributions are accumulating in a special fund, when they are actually being spent as soon as they are collected). They worry that politicians find it too easy to smuggle tax increases past the electorate by disguising them as NICs (as Gordon Brown did in 2001). And they fret that the boundary between contributory benefits and tax-funded welfare has become hopelessly confused.

We shall see that many of these arguments have considerable force. It would be more efficient to means-test the state retirement pension, limiting it to poorer people who actually need the money. They do this in Australia, and the total welfare bill there is much lower as a result. It would also save employers a lot of trouble if they had to calculate a single deduction from their employees' pay packets rather than wrestling with two quite different systems. And combining National Insurance with income tax would make the whole tax and benefits system much simpler for everyone to understand.

The economists are also right when they say that, for most practical purposes, National Insurance operates nowadays just like another layer of income tax. It is a popular misconception that our contributions are kept on deposit somewhere until we need to draw down on them. Ever since the system was set up, the money paid in each week by workers and their employers has immediately been paid out again to a different set of claimants. It might just as well have been collected as income tax.

But the key issue which economists overlook when they conclude that the National Insurance system should be scrapped concerns *fairness*. A system of social security where claims are in principle based on entitlements established by past contributions expresses an important moral rule about how a benefits system should operate, and it is a rule which attracts widespread public commitment. National Insurance is felt intuitively by most people to be a fair way of organising things. We can (and increasingly we do) target needy people quite efficiently by levying taxes on everyone and directing the money at those who most require assistance. But when we organise welfare in this way it attracts nothing like the same depth of public assent as when we pay benefits to those who have themselves contributed towards them.

The contributory principle is simple, we all understand it and it commands widespread support. In Part I of this report, I consider why so many of us feel instinctively that this is a fundamentally fair way of organising things.

I discuss recent research in evolutionary psychology which suggests that the ethic of give-and-take is a product of thousands of years of human (and social) evolution. The result is that most human beings share a common 'gut feeling' about fairness. We know, without being taught, and without necessarily being able to explain or rationalise our sentiments, that we should, as far as possible, put something into the pot if we want to take something out, and that we should not expect others to provide for us if we are capable of providing for ourselves. We also get angry if we see people taking without putting something back.

The 'contributory principle' expresses these instincts that are hard-wired within us. This is why it is so easily understood and broadly supported. The National Insurance system set up after World War II was built on this principle, but it is not the only way it can be given institutional expression. Indeed, we shall see in Part III that there are other, much better ways it might be applied in the modern period. But whatever institutional form it takes, the principle that you pay in before you take out is a vital cornerstone of any welfare system that wants to be regarded by the population as fair as well as decent.

Fairness in social policy matters because it is an essential condition of legitimacy and public consent. Britain's social security system is vast, allocating £207bn in cash benefits and tax credits in 2012/13.[1] A system which processes this much money, equivalent to 23 per cent of the nation's GDP, but which is not widely recognised as operating fairly (with respect to net donors as well as net recipients) will inevitably be undermined by suspicion, envy, fraud and conflict.

Targeted welfare payments financed out of general tax revenues may be efficient in economists' terms, but they are often resented by large sections of the working population that is asked to fund them. This is not because people are selfish or mean-spirited – most of us feel strongly that the genuinely needy must be supported. It is rather because many of us are deeply suspicious of a system that offers people something for nothing, a system that gives without demanding anything back.

Welfare systems which emphasise needs over contributions encourage in everyone else the nagging sense that they are being 'taken for a ride' – that while they are working hard, saving for the future, looking after their families and paying their taxes, other people who are doing none of these things are being supported at their expense. A welfare system that responds only to the problem of need may be efficient, but by rewarding the indigent while penalising the thrifty and hard-working, it can soon appear to contributors to be extremely unfair.

Welfare payments funded out of general taxation worry not only donors. They often make recipients feel uncomfortable too. It is not a pleasant feeling to ask your fellow citizens to put their hands in their pockets because you need their support. It is far better – certainly more empowering – to claim payments which are rightfully yours by virtue of the contributions you have made in the past. The stigma that readily attaches itself to means-tested welfare handouts simply does not arise with contributory benefits. Nobody resents people claiming their own money, and nobody feels guilty drawing down on their own past contributions.

Britain's National Insurance system is in a bad state. The critics are right that far-reaching reforms are needed. But we must not lose sight of the key moral principle that you should, if possible, contribute to your own welfare.

We shall see in Part I how Lloyd George built his unemployment and health insurance reforms before World War I on this contributory principle, just as William Beveridge reinforced it in his comprehensive revamp of the social security system during World War II. Yet in Part II we shall see that our system of social security has increasingly abandoned this principle as the cornerstone of our welfare state.

The challenge is how to reform National Insurance to minimise the many flaws which the critics have identified while at the same time renewing the legacy of the contributory principle on which the system was founded. In Part III we shall work out how this renewal might be achieved, before concluding the report with eight key recommendations for reform.

Hastings, East Sussex
August 2013

PART 1

Fairness and the Contributory Principle

In December 1942, William Beveridge launched his famous report on the future of social insurance in the UK.[1] People reportedly queued all night outside His Majesty's Stationery Office in London to be sure of getting a copy. It sold one hundred thousand copies in its first month, and a shorter summary sold half a million. Nineteen out of twenty people in Britain claimed to have heard about the report, and nearly everyone said they were in favour of its key recommendations.[2] It is impossible to imagine a government report on social security reform attracting this level of public interest and enthusiasm today.

We shall consider Beveridge's specific recommendations, and how they were put into effect, in Part II. For now, we need note only the simple idea at the heart of this report, which was that every worker should pay the same weekly, flat-rate contribution into a new National Insurance scheme. In return, they would be eligible to receive a low but adequate flat-rate benefit if their earnings were interrupted by unemployment, sickness, injury or maternity, and they would qualify for a basic state pension when they reached retirement age.

The plan required everybody who was capable of making

a contribution to do so. In a broadcast for the BBC, Beveridge went to some lengths to emphasise that, while the new system would guarantee people's financial security, he was not proposing that the state should assume responsibility for looking after people's welfare:

> The plan for Britain is based on the contributory principle of giving, not free allowances for all from the State, but benefits as of right in virtue of contributions made by the insured person themselves, as well as by their employer and the State. [3]

As a political liberal, Beveridge thought it important that people should make provision for themselves, and he was wary of doing anything that might undermine the ethic of self-reliance. National Insurance benefits were kept low partly to ensure that everyone could afford to pay for them, but also to encourage those on higher earnings to save or insure on their own account, and not to rely solely on the basic scheme being offered by the government. Benefits were tied to contributions to reinforce the principle that people should take some responsibility for looking after themselves and their dependents, rather than relying on taxpayers to support them when things go wrong.

Beveridge accepted that there would have to be a continuing role for 'National Assistance' – hand-outs from the government, financed by taxpayers – for those who fell upon hard times and who, for one reason or another, had not established a right to benefits through their National Insurance contributions (NICs). But National Assistance was expected to be a last-resort back-up to National Insurance. Beveridge thought most people would never use it. Those who did should be subjected to a financial means test (to ensure they really needed it), and would be expected to comply with various behaviour and good character rules.

Neither of these conditions was to apply to receipt of contributory benefits.

Beveridge wanted National Assistance benefits to be a clearly less desirable alternative to contributory benefits. They could not be set any lower in financial terms, for contributory benefits were themselves only enough to guarantee a basic 'subsistence' income. Indeed, because National Assistance was means-tested on the family's needs, it might even pay more than contributory benefits, which were paid at the same flat rate for everybody. But because contributory benefits had been earned, they were to be paid as of right, with no enquiry into the claimant's financial circumstances, and no probing of their good character. They would not be stigmatised.

Back in 1942, most Britons liked what Beveridge was proposing. Most wanted to look after themselves and their families; they had no desire to be given unearned hand-outs; and they understood and endorsed the contributory principle at the heart of the new National Insurance system. Beveridge's report received widespread public support because the public at that time recognised it as fundamentally *fair*.

The moral dilemma at the heart of welfare

Ever since the English Parliament passed the Poor Law Relief Act in 1601, obliging every parish to levy a poor rate to relieve the suffering of the indigent, the welfare state has been torn between two competing principles.

On the one hand, there has been a commitment to using tax revenues to ensure that people in genuine need are supported rather than being left to suffer. On the other, there has been a concern to maintain the principle of self-reliance by insisting that anyone who can look after themselves and their dependents without outside assistance should do so.

For more than four centuries, these two principles have been undermining each other. The enduring dilemma of welfare policy down the centuries has been how to ensure that people who cannot look after themselves should get help, while at the same time confining assistance to those who genuinely need it. The desire to help those in need leads to more generous welfare, but this in turn encourages more people who could work to claim benefits instead. Politicians then tighten up the eligibility rules and impose more stringent conditions on the receipt of benefits, but this then deters some of those people who really need help from applying for it. And so the dance goes on.

In the modern period, left and right have typically responded to this dilemma by emphasising one objective at the expense of the other:

◆ Socialists and social democrats (the 'left') have generally prioritised compassion. They emphasise the importance of alleviating human need and suffering, even if this becomes increasingly expensive and imposes punitive levels of taxation on those who have to pay for it. There is often a denial that generous or unconditional state welfare discourages self-reliance, but even if it does, this is seen as a price that has to be paid for a decent, inclusive welfare system that looks after all its citizens. The overriding priority is to care for the vulnerable.

◆ On 'the right', conservatives and classical liberals do not deny that people in need have to be helped, but they worry that generous welfare often ends up penalising those who work hard and save (because of the growing tax burden it creates). They also warn that the more generous welfare becomes, the more it is likely to be abused, and there is often a suspicion that many claimants could look after themselves if they really had to. Access to welfare should therefore be made more difficult and demanding, even if this means that some genuinely deserving cases find it harder to get help.

The problem for 'the right' when it engages in these debates is that it sounds heartless. The public may well recognise the validity of many of the claims it makes: we all know there is no bottomless pot; many of us sense that taxes are too high; and most of us know about somebody who is fleecing the welfare system. But pitched against the left's explicitly ethical agenda, the right's much more pragmatic arguments sound mean-spirited. The human urge to be (and – even more important – to be seen to be) caring and compassionate trumps the dull logic of the accounts ledger every time.

The result is that 'fairness' and 'decency' in welfare policy have often been defined exclusively in the terms set by the political 'left', equating fairness with greater equality of outcomes and decency with increased generosity of state benefits. This 'need principle' has come to trump every other consideration in public debates over social policy. Indeed, so rarely is it challenged that many people on the left now seem to believe that theirs is the *only* moral position it is possible to adopt on welfare issues. They attack their opponents on the right, not simply as wrong or misinformed, but as 'uncaring' and even 'immoral'.[4]

For the left, with its overriding morality of need, a proposal to reduce welfare spending is a clear sign of a lack of compassion for people less fortunate than yourself; arguing for lower taxes is an indication of selfishness, greed and excessive individualism; and any attempt to impose stricter eligibility conditions on welfare claimants is a spiteful way of depriving the most vulnerable members of the community of the help they need.

But the arguments coming from the right are not immoral. They are not even amoral. Our moral compass does not begin and end with helping people who are less fortunate than ourselves. Morality and fairness is about more than just compassion. But other ethical concerns relevant to thinking about welfare are often ignored or overlooked in social policy discussions – even by right-wingers. The right is so busy arguing about costs and incentives that it tends to overlook the moral concern that ultimately drives its own arguments.

The ethical principle which the right should be articulating in these debates is just as important as the need principle which the left emphasises. It is a principle which most of us feel just as passionately about. It is the moral principle of 'proportionality', or more simply, the fairness principle appealing to the ideal of just desserts.

Beyond the need principle

When he addressed the public in his radio broadcast in 1942, Beveridge appealed to the moral instincts of his listeners. He spoke in an inspiring way of alleviating need by abolishing the 'five giant evils' of squalor, ignorance, want, idleness and disease. But he also spoke eloquently about maintaining the ethic of self-reliance in the new National Insurance system by requiring everyone to contribute as a condition of claiming benefits.

Beveridge explicitly appealed to the deep-seated belief among members of the public that people should look ahead and take whatever steps are necessary to support themselves and their dependents (by saving for a rainy day, or insuring against calamitous risks), rather than relying on the generosity of their neighbours to help them out when things go wrong. This is the essence of the fairness principle, that we should not free-ride on the generosity of other people.

Where did this idea of fairness originate? According to the American evolutionary psychologist Jonathon Haidt we do not have to learn it from other people or from books, for it is universal across all human societies. It is an instinctive feeling that has been hard-wired within us as a result of thousands of years of human and social evolution.

In his book *The Righteous Mind,* Haidt discusses a number of psychology experiments indicating that almost all humans share some very basic and innate 'gut feelings' (he calls them 'intuitions') about how to behave.[5] He suggests that these intuitions evolved over hundreds of thousands of years as natural selection favoured those of our ancestors who knew without having to think too much how to respond quickly and appropriately to the behaviour of others.

If his theory is correct, it means that our fundamental rules governing right and wrong behaviour are not arbitrary or artificial, but reflect deeply-embedded moral instincts. As Haidt emphasises, it also means that people who express different political or religious ideals from our own may be no less moral than we are: it is just that they are prioritising different moral instincts among those we all share from those that we choose to emphasise.[6]

Down the centuries, philosophers have tried to explain morality logically, by deriving rules from a few basic axioms (e.g. the idea that something is wrong if it harms others). But Haidt says philosophy has been looking at things the wrong way around. Our brains are already wired to tell us what is good and bad, right and wrong. It is only since we developed the use of language that we have started reflecting on why we feel the way we do. Using language, we select arguments that fit our intuitions, which is where the philosophers come in. But these ethical theories are merely confirming what is already there. They are not discovering anything we don't already feel. Core elements of human morality are grounded in instinct, not reason.

Haidt does not deny that social groups differ in their cultural norms and values, nor that infants and children have to be taught the specific rules of their particular society. But we are all born with instinctive feelings about the right and wrong way to behave, and the formal laws and social norms of the particular societies we are born into are mapped onto these intuitions in the course of our socialisation. Haidt doesn't just assert this; he demonstrates it, drawing on a wide range of experimental and other evidence.

For example, he cites research on six-month old infants who are shown a puppet struggling to get up a hill. A second figure is introduced, which tries to help the puppet's efforts to climb the hill, and a third, which does its best to hinder them. Given the choice afterwards of which of these two additional figures to cuddle, infants invariably select the helpful one, and if the climbing puppet is later shown embracing the hinderer, infants stare perplexed, for this is not what their brains are hard-wired to expect.

As early as six months, long before parents or school teachers can teach us the appropriate rules or reason with us about why something is the right course of action, it seems most of us already know it is right to help and care for others, and wrong to hinder them for no reason. We feel this morality in our bones.[7] Haidt calls this gut feeling the 'care instinct'. It corresponds more-or-less to what I earlier identified as the need principle in social welfare, the moral rule that says we should help those who need our assistance.

How did this care instinct evolve? Haidt notes that Bentham tried to explain it by his utilitarian ethics (helping others maximises aggregate human happiness). Kant tried to explain it with his categorical imperative (pure reason dictates that we should treat others as we would wish to be treated ourselves, which means helping rather than harming them). But Haidt says it derives, not from abstract principles like these, but from an evolved need for humans to protect and care for children who cannot survive without nurturing. Quite simply, those of our ancestors who lacked this instinct are likely to have died without successfully bringing their children to maturity, leaving those with more compassionate genes to pass them on successfully to the next generation.

Once this 'care instinct' had evolved, it could be mobilised by all sorts of other stimuli in addition to needy children. In many western societies, for example, people often feel compassion for furry animals, or even for cartoon characters. Signs of 'cuteness' can trigger a strong urge to care, nurture and protect whenever we encounter them, even if they have become wholly disassociated from children. So while the impulse to help and protect is rooted in the instinct to care for your own children, it has been generalised out to apply to a variety of different situations which vary between cultures and groups.[8]

The 'care instinct' is only one of six 'moral foundations' identified in Haidt's book. According to him, not only do we have a natural urge to look after the weak and defenceless ('care'), but we also naturally feel rage against people who don't pull their weight (what he calls the 'proportionality' or fairness instinct). We also react against being dominated and pushed around (the 'liberty' instinct), although we share an acute sense of hierarchy ('authority') and have strong feelings of responsibility to the group ('loyalty'). We also have an instinctive feeling of revulsion and awe triggered by exposure to certain symbols and objects in our environment (what Haidt calls 'sanctity'). All of these instincts evolved as adaptive solutions to the struggle for individual and group survival.

What is of most interest for an understanding of public sentiments about welfare is that, in addition to the care instinct, we all also share a proportionality or 'fairness instinct'. Just as experimental psychologists have demonstrated the existence of the care instinct, so (very convincingly) they have also demonstrated our fierce and intuitive commitment to a fairness instinct.

Game theorists have known for a long time that the most effective and enduringly successful strategy for interacting with others in any group context is 'tit-for-tat'. In other words, if you want to get the most advantageous outcome for yourself, as well as for other people, the way to do it is to start off co-operating with them, and to keep co-operating for as long as your goodwill is reciprocated. However, as soon as the other party fails to reciprocate, you must retaliate to avoid being exploited by other people concerned only with their own wellbeing. Maintaining consistency in your pattern of response sends a clear signal to others that while you are open to mutual endeavour, you cannot be exploited. Once their co-operation resumes, you should immediately reciprocate, thereby restoring the joint advantage to be enjoyed by mutual co-operation. Nothing is to be gained by harbouring grudges.

Robert Axelrod, who first demonstrated the efficacy and robustness of this tit-for-tat strategy by running repeated computer simulations of competing strategies, summarises the winning formula as: 'being nice, retaliatory, forgiving and clear'.[9] We start off by trusting strangers to reciprocate, treating them as we hope to be treated ourselves (being 'nice'). But if they break this trust, we respond in like manner (being 'retaliatory'). If they mend their ways, we resume co-operation (being 'forgiving'). And we always follow these rules (being 'clear').

Haidt is aware of Axelrod's findings. As he puts it: 'We co-operate with those who have been nice to us, and we shun those who took advantage of us.'[10] But what he adds to Axelrod's key insight is that tit-for-tat not only generally delivers the optimal result; it also feels right and appropriate to most people. According to Haidt, this is because it corresponds to an intuitive sense of fair behaviour that is the product of human and social evolution. Tit-for-tat, in other words, is not simply an effective strategy to adopt in group situations; it is an evolved, instinctive moral rule that all of us are pre-programmed to recognise and respect.

How do we know this is an evolved instinct? We can start by demonstrating it logically, for those of our ancestors who always took from those around them but never gave (non-co-operators) would soon have been shunned by the group and are unlikely to have survived, while those who gave unconditionally to anyone who asked (non-retaliators) would have been mercilessly exploited by the group, and are likewise unlikely to have flourished. Evolution will have favoured those with a deeply-ingrained sense of fairness as proportionality – the gut sense that people should be rewarded in proportion to what they have contributed to the interaction.

We can demonstrate this instinct experimentally too. Haidt reports some recent research that shows, not only that many of us feel committed to the fairness principle, but also that we are desperate for others to recognise it too, so much so that we may be willing to act quite irrationally to ensure that they do.

Researchers set up a game in which each player was given a sum of money and told they could choose whether to contribute some or all of this money to a common pot. At the end of each round, the pot was supplemented according to how much in total had been contributed, and the total amount was then distributed equally among the players. It was therefore in everybody's interest that group members should contribute generously, for this maximised everybody's potential gain.

However, team members were changed between each round. This prevented shared norms of trust or reciprocity from evolving through application of tit-for-tat strategies. You could not build up a reputation as a good team member, because the composition of your team kept changing. Nor would you run any risk of reprisals if you held back your contributions and benefited from everybody else's generosity, because in each round you could free-ride on a fresh and unsuspecting set of players. This situation was set up to reward selfish behaviour and penalise co-operation.

The rational strategy for any player under these circumstances was to contribute nothing to the communal pot and free-ride in each round on the contributions of others. They could only gain by this, for there could be no come-back from those whose generosity they exploited. But the researchers found this is not what most participants did. Rather, they continued to contribute at each round, but the size of their contributions started to fall as they experienced successive instances of free-riders benefiting from their continued generosity.

At this point, the researchers introduced a new rule which allowed players to pay to have others penalised for not contributing to the pot. Again, the rational strategy was never to pay to have others punished, for the players continued to change at the end of each round, so it was impossible to gain from any reformed behaviour your punishment may have brought about in others. Yet despite this, 84 per cent of participants in this experiment did pay to punish free-riders.

They did so for deeply-held moral reasons – they were furious that free-riders were behaving unethically, and they were prepared to lose out themselves if it meant justice would be done to the cheats. As Haidt explains: 'We hate to see people take without giving. We want to see cheaters and slackers "get what's coming to them". We want the law of karma to run its course, and we're willing to help enforce it.'[11]

Interestingly, once participants were allowed to pay to have free-riders punished, the value of contributions to the communal pots skyrocketed in later rounds. It turns out that incurring costs yourself in order to inflict deserved punishment on free-riders not only makes you feel better, but it makes economic sense too, for it shifts the moral climate in favour of greater co-operation. Group co-operation and beneficial collective outcomes strengthen when free-riders are no longer allowed to get away scot free. Punishing free-riders promotes virtue and benefits the collectivity, while indulging them encourages selfishness all round and swiftly erodes group cohesion.[12]

The lessons for the organisation of modern social welfare systems seem all too obvious. The caring instinct drives us to offer help to others in need, but the fairness instinct requires that we deter and punish free-riders. This requires that receiving help should normally be conditional on having made prior contributions (or failing that, on repayment of benefits at a later date). Ignoring this reciprocity rule will not only generate a justifiable sense of grievance among those who are pulling their weight, but it will quickly threaten the viability of the whole system as people become less and less willing to keep contributing and cooperating.

Beveridge was alive to this danger. Many on the left today, however, seem blind to it.

Compassion *and* fairness

Haidt describes his own politics as 'progressive', but he worries that conservative ethics seem to be more comprehensive (and therefore more in tune with fully-rounded human nature) than social democratic and socialist ones. The universal foundations of human morality are built, he says, on all six of the evolved instincts he identifies, and conservatism more-or-less expresses all six. It cares about the weak (albeit sometimes rather patronisingly); it abhors free-riders; it respects authority; it emphasises the rights and liberties of the individual; it is patriotic (group loyalty); and it venerates the traditional symbolism of religion and other 'sacred' institutions inherited from the past.

The left, by contrast, seems in modern western societies to barely recognise more than two of these moral instincts.[13] Haidt says leftists feel the 'care' instinct very strongly, which is why their rhetoric and programmes echo with calls for compassion for those who are less fortunate. They also emphasise the 'liberty' instinct in their hostility to big capitalist corporations and their support for minority rights and alternative lifestyles. But there is little room in modern left-wing sentiment for the authority instinct (doing as you are told), the loyalty instinct (putting your own group or nation first), or the sanctity instinct (the religious sense of being part of something bigger and more important than yourself). Most importantly for our current concerns, the proportionality instinct (ensuring people don't take what they don't deserve) is also only weakly expressed and appreciated in most left-wing discourse.

The implication is not only that conservatism seems better placed to express the full range of people's sense of what is right, but also that the right understands where the left is coming from far better than the left understands the right. Conservatives may be a bit less compassionate than socialists and social democrats, but their ideological concerns straddle all six moralities, which means they can understand where their opponents are coming from. In contrast, ideologues on the left seem incapable of appreciating the moral basis of many conservative arguments.[14]

If Haidt is correct, this would help explain why the left so often believes that it alone is arguing from moral principle. It is because it simply doesn't recognise or understand the moral principles being expressed by its opponents.

More importantly, Haidt's analysis also strongly suggests that the left's familiar social policy agenda – the concern to alleviate poverty, flatten income inequalities and support the vulnerable – must be supplemented by other concerns more often expressed from the right if welfare provision is to reflect a more rounded sense of human morality. In particular, while our caring instinct dictates that we help those in need, we should listen to our fairness instinct when deciding how to do it.

Need, fairness and public opinion

Any ethical welfare policy must ensure that people in need have support if they cannot support themselves. British public opinion strongly endorses this.

Polling by Ipsos-MORI in 2012 found that around 90 per cent of the British public agrees in principle that there should be a welfare system that provides a safety net for anyone who needs it.[15] In another 2012 survey for the BBC, ConRes asked a sample of the British public if everyone should have the right to a minimum standard of living guaranteed if necessary by welfare payments, and 72 per cent thought they should while only 18 per cent disagreed.[16]

But the ethics of state welfare go beyond this. Policy has also to be fair (not just to recipients, but to donors as well), and public opinion in Britain strongly endorses this fairness principle too.

Research by Policy Exchange in 2011 found that 'fairness' is a major concern of the British public (it ranked second only to 'economic responsibility' when people were asked what values they look for in a political party). The study confirmed that when people endorse 'fairness' as a principle, they are mainly referring to what Haidt called 'proportionality', or the ideal of just desserts. Asked what they meant by 'fairness', 63 per cent said that 'fairness is about getting what you deserve', while only 26 per cent thought 'fairness is about equality'.[17]

Applied to welfare policy, 'getting what you deserve' means limiting benefits to those who really need them, and ensuring that if people claiming benefits are capable of working, they are required to do something in return.

Thus, the same Ipsos-MORI survey that found 90 per cent public support for a welfare safety net also found that 84 per cent of people want stricter tests for incapacity benefits, and 78 per cent think the unemployed should take any job that is offered to them.[18] These are sentiments about fairness – that people should not get disability payments if they are capable of working, and should not get unemployment payments if they are unwilling to take the jobs that are available.

There is also a strong belief among the British public that welfare recipients should do something to earn their benefits. The Policy Exchange research found 80 per cent support (with just 13 per cent disagreeing) for the idea that people who are capable of working but who have been out of work for a year or more should be required to undertake a work activity in return for their benefits. Support for this principle was strong across all social classes and supporters of all political parties. As the report concluded: 'The notion of "something for something" is very strong ' among the British public.[19]

Four fairness rules

From Haidt's moral principle of 'proportionality', it is possible to derive four key rules which should be addressed when assessing the fairness of any welfare policy or proposal.

First, fairness demands that people should take responsibility for themselves and their dependents before requesting assistance from strangers. Sometimes, there is no other option but to request state support, but as Beveridge said in respect of National Assistance, it should always be the last resort. If possible, people should 'stand on their own two feet.'

Public opinion strongly endorses this sentiment. A YouGov poll in September 2010 found that 82 per cent of Britons support cutting benefits for claimants who refuse jobs, while only eight per cent oppose it.[20] An Ipsos MORI poll in May 2010 found 60 per cent think 'people who refuse the offer of a job should not be allowed state benefits, regardless of their personal circumstances'. Only 29 per cent disagreed with this.[21] So if work is available, you should take it, rather than rely on assistance from taxpayers.

The second fairness rule requires that those who do get state assistance should not end up in a better position than people who are working. This obviously means that benefits should not make them better off financially than people who are in work (something the Coalition government has tried to ensure with the new Universal Credit and the benefits cap). But it also means that people on benefits should not be given perks (like enrolment in free training courses) which people in work would have to pay for, and that the demands made on them as a condition of receiving their benefits should be no less onerous than the demands made on people who work to earn an income.

The 1834 English Poor Law took this second fairness rule very seriously and expressed it in the idea of 'less eligibility'.[22] Less eligibility meant that the situation of the lowest-paid worker should always be better than that of a comparable person in receipt of state aid. This applied to the use of their time as well as the amount of money they received, which is why recipients of state aid were often put to work as a condition of receiving financial assistance.

Because of the harsh conditions in some nineteenth century workhouses, this principle of less eligibility gradually became tarnished. But the fact that it was applied harshly does not mean it should not be applied at all. Today, we are belatedly rediscovering its importance as we once again seek to attach activity conditions ('workfare') to receipt of certain welfare benefits. Public opinion strongly endorses this. A BBC Radio 4 poll in November 2012 found 84 per cent of people agree that 'people who are able to work should be required to do so in order to receive benefits'.[23] Most people think it is only fair that if other people are working to pay for your benefits, you should be expected to do something too.

Third, fairness involves discrimination. Everyone in need must be able to access help, but the conditions attached to receipt of assistance should vary according to the circumstances of particular claims. Those who knowingly or recklessly contribute to their own misfortune, for example, should not expect the same treatment as those who encounter problems through no fault of their own. If they want help, they must change their behaviour.

Again, the welfare system used to make such distinctions. When taxpayer-funded old-age pensions were first introduced by Lloyd George, for example, they were restricted to those whose conduct marked them as 'deserving', and until 1919, criminals, drunkards and malingerers were excluded.[24] In the 1940s too, Beveridge wanted national assistance made conditional on behaviour, although not much came of the idea.

Today, however, we are squeamish about judging the behaviour of others, and left-wing social policy orthodoxy fiercely resists any attempt to distinguish the 'deserving' from the 'undeserving'. But clearly, not all welfare claimants are equally deserving of help. Our instinctive sense of fairness tells us that people who engage in anti-social or self-destructive behaviour deserve less sympathy than those who fall victim to circumstances beyond their control, and yet again, this is reflected in public opinion.

IPSOS-Mori reported in 2010, for example, that 51 per cent of people think parents who fail to bring up their children properly should lose their family payments, and only 26 per cent disagreed.[25] A 2008 survey found 89 per cent of the British public thought drug users should only get welfare benefits if they submit to treatment for their addiction, with only four per cent opposing this (although left-wing experts predictably worry that such a policy might deter addicts from claiming benefits).[26] It is unfair on those who behave responsibly to treat them the same as those who do not.

Finally, as we have already noted, fairness requires that if you want to take something out of the pot, you must put something back in. People earn a right to support if they have contributed to a savings scheme, or paid into an insurance policy, and this marks them out from those who have failed to safeguard themselves against future mishaps. The care instinct tells us that everyone in need should be eligible for help, but the fairness instinct dictates that people should reap as they sow.

This fourth fairness rule is the one William Beveridge appealed to in his radio broadcast to the British public back in 1942. It requires that we all save and insure ourselves and our dependents to minimise the likelihood of our becoming a charge on other people. This rule goes to the heart of the fairness instinct, identified by Haidt, for it aims to enforce personal responsibility and keep free-riding to a minimum. It is this rule with which we shall be mainly concerned for the remainder of this report, although we shall encounter all four rules again as we consider what has gone wrong with our social security system, and how we might put it right.

PART II

The Corrosion of National Insurance

Ever since Lloyd George introduced compulsory state unemployment and health insurance back in 1911, the UK system of social security has been based (at least notionally) on the principle that people should establish an entitlement to financial support from the state by making regular contributions to a 'National Insurance Fund.' We pay into a fund while we are working so that we can draw on it when our earnings are interrupted as a result of factors like unemployment, sickness, child birth or retirement.

This 'contributory principle' of National Insurance is simple, fair and easily understood. Provided you have paid your contributions (still often popularly referred to by older people as the 'National Insurance stamp'), you have a right to a range of benefits, including unemployment pay if you lose your job, sickness pay if you are too ill to work, an incapacity payment if you become permanently incapable of working, a maternity allowance if you stop work to have a baby, and a government pension once you reach retirement age.

There is no means test attached to receipt of any of these benefits, for your past payments into the fund establish your right to claim from it when relevant conditions arise, irrespective of your current financial circumstances. The state does not give you these benefits because it thinks you need the money, or it sees you as a deserving case; it pays them because your contributions record gives you the right to claim them when certain events happen in your life. This is why little stigma or shame has ever been associated with receiving insured benefits, for claimants are not soliciting other people's help or charity. They are claiming what is theirs by right, as in any insurance-based contract.

Because not everyone is in paid work, not everyone is in a position to pay National Insurance contributions. This means that, underpinning the system of contributory benefits, we have always also needed a social security safety net for those who haven't been working, haven't paid into the National Insurance fund, and have therefore failed to create any entitlements. As we shall see, this safety net has also supported insured workers who use up all their entitlements, and those (such as unemployed workers with large families) who find their insured benefits are inadequate for their needs and who therefore need a top-up.

This back-up system has taken a number of forms over the last hundred years. It originated as Poor Law relief, which was replaced in 1934 by National (or Public) Assistance, which in turn gave way in the sixties to Supplementary Benefit and, later, Income Support. Now, yet another change is being introduced with the introduction of Universal Credit, a new benefit which combines income support with various other means-tested payments including income-based Jobseeker's Allowance, income-based Employment and Support Allowance, child tax credits, working tax credits and housing benefit.[1]

Throughout each of these incarnations, safety net payments have been funded out of general taxation rather than prior contributions. This has given them a very different character from National Insurance, and we see this reflected in the negative sentiments commonly expressed both by those who claim these benefits, and by those who find themselves paying for them through their taxes.

Because uninsured assistance in its various forms has always been financed by tax revenues, claimants cannot be said to have done anything to establish a 'right' to this money. They get it because they are deemed to need help, not because they have contributed in the past to a common fund. For this reason, this kind of assistance has always been subject to some kind of means test, for payments are only made to people who can demonstrate they are in need and have little or no money of their own to draw upon. These means tests have often been resented by claimants who find it demeaning to have to prove to officials that they need help.

Uninsured assistance has also often been tied to certain behavioural conditions. At various times in the last hundred years, it has been limited to claimants 'of good character', to those who are married, to those who can prove they have 'genuinely' been seeking work, and to those who agree to undertake training or work experience programmes. While the application of a means test seeks to limit aid to those who really 'need' it, the imposition of behavioural or activity conditions aims to reassure taxpayers that aid is being directed only to those who really 'deserve' it.

Because they have established no 'right' to support, recipients of non-contributory benefits have often felt tainted by a sense of personal shame or social stigma when they make a claim (in the past, although one suspects much less now, people in dire need were sometimes too proud to ask for the help they needed). Conversely, taxpayers who have been required to pay for these benefits have often expressed suspicion or downright hostility towards those who claim them, as in the widespread belief (justified or not) that a significant proportion of claimants are 'scrounging' or 'shirking'.

A survey conducted for BBC Radio 4 in November 2012 asked a sample of the British public what proportion of welfare claimants they think lie about their circumstances in order to get benefits, or refuse to work even when jobs are available. Fewer than 10 per cent of the public thought that only 'a tiny number, if any' fell into this category; 40 per cent thought it was half or more of all claimants.[2] A 2013 YouGov poll for *The Sunday Times* found that four-fifths of voters believe there are 'significant numbers of undeserving benefit claimants', and nearly two-thirds thought the welfare system is too lax in determining who gets benefits.[3]

People who feel they have 'done the right thing' by working, saving and building up entitlements resent being 'taken for a ride' by other people who they believe could work but who choose to claim benefits instead. Often, those who feel most resentment are the people with little money themselves, people who struggle to get by while seeing their neighbours living on benefits.[4]

These negative sentiments are strongly rooted in the 'fairness/cheating' instinct identified in Part I. People have an intuitive sense of the fairness of a system of contributory benefits, where you take out only if you have paid in, but non-contributory welfare does not measure up to this. Faced with people in need, our compassionate instincts prompt us to want to help, but anger and resentment surface at the first suspicion that claimants are free-riding and exploiting our good nature.

The 'contributory principle', embedded in the system of National Insurance, expresses our instinct for fairness (proportionality) because it explicitly requires that people should put something into the collective pot before they take something out of it. This suggests that welfare policy should try to ensure that people who have made a prior contribution are treated more favourably than those who have done little or nothing to safeguard their futures.

Rather than safeguarding and strengthening this crucial contributory principle, however, successive governments have allowed it to be gradually eroded, with the result that the basic principle of fairness in our welfare system has been undermined. Increasingly, the welfare state has come to concern itself simply with the relief of need, with little regard for the equally important question of fair treatment for all. In this part of this essay, we shall trace how this neglect of fairness came about, leaving to Part III a consideration of the ways in which the contributory principle might be restored.

Establishing a right to benefits: National Insurance

During the nineteenth century, working-class families in Britain commonly made their own welfare arrangements. Millions of workers voluntarily insured themselves and their families against loss of earnings, either by buying commercial insurance policies or by joining mutual, friendly societies. Although most of those who bought cover were in skilled trades offering regular employment, they also included a number of less skilled and lower-paid workers. By 1910 (just before Lloyd George introduced the country's first compulsory state health and unemployment insurance scheme) there were 26,877 friendly societies in Britain offering sickness and medical benefits to more than six and a half million members.[5]

When Lloyd George introduced the compulsory state health and unemployment insurance scheme, he built on the foundations of these existing, voluntary schemes. Part I of the 1911 National Insurance Act (which dealt with health insurance) required workers to join an 'approved' scheme run by a friendly society. Employees had to pay 4*d.* per week, which was supplemented by 3*d.* from their employer and 2*d.* from the government. In return, they had the right to 10*s.* per week sick pay, plus free medical treatment from a doctor belonging to a local panel.[6] Although the government mandated and subsidised health insurance after 1911, it was the friendly societies that continued to administer it.

Part II of the 1911 Act introduced compulsory unemployment insurance for more than two million workers employed in industries like building, ship and vehicle construction, mechanical engineering and iron founding, which were seen as peculiarly susceptible to periodic booms and slumps in the economy. Employees and employers were each required to make weekly contributions of 2½*d.*, topped up by 1⅔*d.* from the government, in return for which workers were given an entitlement to 7*s.* per week unemployment benefit for a maximum of fifteen weeks.[7] Unlike health insurance, this unemployment cover was run by the state, not the voluntary sector. The Act also introduced state-run Employment Exchanges to help unemployed workers find new jobs.

While sickness and unemployment were covered by this early national insurance scheme, retirement was not. In 1908, the government introduced a basic old-age pension, but unlike health and unemployment benefits, this was non-contributory and was funded out of general taxation. Everybody over seventy was covered. From the very beginning, the cost to taxpayers proved heavier than had been anticipated: pensions cost £8 million in the first year, compared with an estimate of £6.5 million.[8]

In 1925, Neville Chamberlain's Widows', Orphans' and Old Age Contributory Pensions Act extended the contributory principle to retirement pensions by bringing them (partially) into the national insurance system. Levying equal contributions on employers and employees (with a variable contribution from the state), it provided a five-year, non-means-tested pension for insured workers once they reached the age of 65, together with benefits for widows and children of those who died. At 70, retirees transferred to the existing, tax-financed old-age pension (although life expectancy at that time meant many never reached 70). In 1937, this partial contributory scheme was extended to cover white-collar as well as manual workers, but pensions did not become fully integrated into National Insurance until after World War II.

The short economic boom at the end of World War I allowed the unemployment insurance fund to build up a surplus of £21 million, and in 1920 this emboldened the government to extend the scheme to cover virtually all workers earning less than £250 per year. Soon after that, however, the fund's surplus evaporated as unemployment started to rise. Through the 1920s, jobless men struggled to find new jobs within the 15-week insurance window, with the result that increasing numbers of them were thrown back onto the old Poor Law as their eligibility for Unemployment Benefit expired. As governments came up with a series of ad hoc responses to extend people's insurance cover, they began to drive the first nails into the contributory principle's coffin.

Of particular significance was the introduction of so-called 'uncovenanted benefits' for those who had exhausted their 15 week entitlement. These were notionally 'advances' to be repaid out of future contributions once recipients returned to work, but these 'loans' were largely fictional, for much of the money was never recouped. Uncovenanted benefits were essentially taxpayer-funded assistance masquerading as contributory insurance.

In 1927, the 15-week time limit on receipt of contributory unemployment benefit was removed altogether. This meant benefits could be claimed indefinitely provided *some* prior contribution had been made.[9] And in the same year, a new, taxpayer-funded 'transitional benefit' was introduced for those who had no contributions record, effectively severing altogether the link between benefits and contributions.

William Beveridge, who was at that time the Director of the London School of Economics, was appalled by this drift away from the contributory principle. He later complained to Winston Churchill about the Conservative government of 1927 which had 'made the insurance benefit unlimited in time and formally divorced the claim to benefit from payment of contributions'.[10]

In 1934, a new Unemployment Act sought to re-establish a clear dividing line between unemployment insurance and assistance given to uninsured claimants. Part I of the Act extended compulsory unemployment insurance to cover almost everyone (15 million workers). It also restructured the balance of contributions (one-third each from employees, employers and government) and set up an independent statutory body to run the system as a self-financing scheme. The entire fund was ring-fenced so that none of it could be used to pay benefits to people who had no entitlements or who had exhausted their benefits.

Part II of the Act dealt with assistance to the uninsured unemployed (then numbering around one million). They became the responsibility of a new Unemployment Assistance Board, funded by the taxpayer, which could make National Assistance payments based on its assessment of families' needs. This Board later became the National Assistance Board after it assumed responsibility for paying supplementary pensions to retired people and widows, as well as unemployment assistance.

By the outbreak of World War II, 60 per cent of the unemployed were receiving insured benefits with 32 per cent on National Assistance and the remainder receiving local assistance through the remnants of the old Poor Law.[11]

It was this dual system of insured benefits on the one hand, and means-tested assistance on the other, that Beveridge sought to reinforce and extend in his famous 1942 report. Specifically, he wanted to bolster the insurance component for retired, sick and unemployed workers while relegating uninsured National Assistance to a residual safety net function.

His report proposed a simple, flat-rate weekly contribution (with a lower rate levied on married women and young workers)[12] in return for an unconditional entitlement to a range of flat-rate benefits (which again were lower for young people and married women). In addition to covering unemployment, these benefits included sickness, medical, funeral, industrial injury, maternity, and widows' and orphans' payments, plus the old-age pension (which was renamed the 'retirement pension' and would be fully incorporated into the National Insurance system). Regardless of their wage level, all workers would pay the same weekly amount and would receive the same level of benefit.

There was to be no means-testing of any of these payments (for they were earned as of right), but benefits would be set at a fairly low 'subsistence' level so there would still be an incentive for workers to make their own provisions over and above the basic minimum provided by the state. Insured benefits, said Beveridge, should be 'high enough to provide subsistence to prevent want', but not so high that they might deter work or voluntary provision. Those who wanted a better level of cover could make their own, additional, private arrangements.

As a Liberal, Beveridge believed in self-reliance, and he rejected what he saw as the 'socialistic' idea that everyone should be supported out of general tax revenues.[13] He believed (probably correctly) that public opinion was similarly hostile to unearned doles, and that most people strongly favoured thrift and endorsed the principle that benefits should be earned.[14] As we saw in Part I, he even reassured the public in a BBC broadcast that his plan was not offering 'free allowances for all from the State', but was establishing a right to benefits 'in virtue of contributions made by the insured person themselves'.[15]

For those who, for whatever reason, had not established a contributions record, National Assistance would still be available, but Beveridge expected it to dwindle in significance. Provided reasonably full employment were maintained in the post-war economy, he thought most workers would build up a strong enough contributions record to give them a full state pension when they retired, and to cover any brief periods of unemployment.[16]

Beveridge recognised that a fundamental weakness of his social insurance model was that the flat-rate weekly contribution would have to be low enough for the lowest-paid workers to afford it. This meant benefits would have to be low too, otherwise the fund would go bust. The problem with this was that although a low level of benefit might be adequate for childless claimants who found themselves between jobs for a short period, it could plainly prove a problem for unemployed or sick workers with large numbers of children to support.

Beveridge's answer to this was a new system of non-means-tested 'family allowances' to be paid to employed and unemployed families alike. He thought that helping all families with the cost of raising their children would allow unemployment and other insured benefits to be kept low without driving families into destitution. This would then obviate the need for insured workers to seek top-ups from means-tested National Assistance and would avoid the problem that had arisen before the war when those on means-tested public assistance had sometimes received

THE CORROSION OF NATIONAL INSURANCE

more than those claiming insured benefits.

A further problem was that if insured benefits were to be paid at subsistence level, they would not be worth any more than uninsured National Assistance payments (for the basic safety net could not be set below subsistence). This seems to defeat the whole point of insurance – why pay contributions into an insurance fund when those with no contributions still qualify for the same amount of assistance from taxpayers? To deal with this, Beveridge insisted that National Assistance should be differentiated from insured benefits by making it subject to a means test and to certain behavioural conditions:

> It must be felt to be something less desirable than insurance benefit; otherwise the insured person gets nothing for their contributions. Assistance therefore will be given subject always to proof of needs and examination of means; it will be subject also to any conditions as to behaviour which may seem likely to hasten restoration of earning capacity. [17]

So while insured benefits would be no more generous than National Assistance, they would still be more desirable because they were exempt from means-testing and (though only for the first six months, in the case of Unemployment Insurance) from conditionality.[18] In this way, Beveridge's scheme hoped to fulfil the less eligibility requirement we identified as a basic fairness rule in Part I.

The flaws in the post-war National Insurance scheme

Beveridge's plan was implemented in the 1946 National Insurance Act, but with a number of significant amendments. First, although Beveridge recommended that the new state retirement pension fund should be built up over twenty years, so an adequate amount of money could accumulate before pensions started to be paid out, this advice was ignored.[19] Instead, the post-war Labour government introduced the new pensions immediately (16s per week for men over 65 and women over 60). This meant there would be no 'pensions fund' from which retirees would be paid. Instead, the system would have to be financed on a 'pay-as-you-go' basis, paying pensioners not from their own past contributions, but from those being paid currently by younger people still in the workforce.[20]

Although many workers believed (and apparently still nowadays believe)[21] that they were depositing their NI contributions in a pot from which they would later draw their pension, the truth is that there never has been a pot. Instead, National Insurance has been run like a giant, government-sponsored, Ponzi scheme.[22] Each week, one group's fresh contributions have been used to pay another's pensions. As Aneurin Bevan, Minister for Health in the post-war Labour government, candidly observed: 'The great secret about the National Insurance fund is that there ain't no fund.'[23]

Beveridge's original insurance principle was thus deeply compromised right from the start, and given that retirement pensions have always represented the biggest single item in the National Insurance budget, this was a major flaw. As the population has aged, the scheme has come under ever-increasing pressure, for more and more retirees now depend on revenues extracted from those still working.

A second significant change concerned Beveridge's suggestion that insured benefits for workers below retirement age should be paid indefinitely, for so long as their need continued. This was rejected for fear that it could be open to abuse. Instead, the standard period of insured unemployment benefits was limited to 180 working days

(30 weeks), although claimants with strong contribution records could claim 'additional days' up to a full year, and tribunals could grant 'extended benefit' for a further six months beyond that.[24] Once insured benefits had finally run out, however, claimants would have to rely on National Assistance, just as they had under the old, pre-war system. They would only become eligible for further unemployment benefit after they had found work and paid another 13 weeks of NI stamps.

As things turned out, most unemployment spells in the early years of the scheme were short-term, so very few insured claimants ran out of eligibility. In the early fifties, 83 per cent of unemployment benefit claimants got back into work within three weeks, and 98 per cent found jobs within six months. Even in the 1960s, the average length of unemployment was still less than ten weeks.[25]

But despite this, National Assistance never dwindled to the secondary role that Beveridge had envisaged for it. The reason was that, even with the new family allowances, insured benefits were not high enough to guarantee 'adequate subsistence' for everyone. This meant that, right from the outset, a minority of insured claimants – mainly those with substantial family responsibilities – had to be given National Assistance top-ups.

Because it was means-tested, National Assistance took account of factors like the number of dependents in a household and the amount of rent people had to pay, whereas unemployment benefit was paid at a flat rate to everyone. Every year between 1950 and 1978, around one-fifth of those receiving contributory Unemployment Benefit also got taxpayer-funded National Assistance (or later, 'supplementary benefit') top-ups.[26] Once high rates of unemployment returned in the 1970s, and the number of people out of work for long periods escalated, increasing numbers came to rely on National Assistance as they ran out of entitlement. The residualisation of uninsured, means-tested benefits which Beveridge had envisaged never happened.

A third change was that successive post-war governments retreated from any serious commitment to conditionality when granting National Assistance. Beveridge's insistence that uninsured benefits should be made strongly conditional, in order to differentiate them from insured benefits of the same value, was never implemented effectively.[27] The expectation that claimants should be 'of good character' was not enforced, and although the unemployed have in principle always been required to look for work, this condition has often been neglected in practice.[28] A related problem is that jobless people have increasingly claimed income support on grounds of disability or caring (usually parenting) responsibilities, rather than registering as unemployed, and, until recently, this has exempted them from any conditions (including any obligation to look for work).

There were other flaws, too, in the Beveridge blueprint. His hope that workers would supplement their state benefits through additional, voluntary payments into private savings, insurance and pension schemes never took off. Today, almost seventy years on, less than one person in eight is covered by private health insurance, and in most cases this is paid for by their employers.[29] Even fewer insure against future nursing home or elderly care costs; private unemployment or redundancy insurance (other than payment protection policies linked to mortgages and credit cards) is rare; and we are still as a nation wrestling with the problem that millions of people of working age fail to make adequate provision for their retirement.

Nor did Beveridge foresee the catastrophic impact on his scheme of the revolution in family life – what Francis Fukuyama has called the 'Great Disruption' – that exploded in most western societies between the 1960s and the 1990s.[30]

In the world for which Beveridge devised his plan, children were generally reared by married parents and divorce was rare. In most cases, the father worked while the mother stayed at home looking after the house and raising the children. Because couples rarely separated, and few women had children outside of marriage, most mature women and children were supported by male wage-earners covered by the National Insurance scheme. Married women relied on the earnings, and shared in the entitlements, of their husbands.

Given this context, Beveridge's principal concern was simply to ensure that families could get by when their male wage-earner lost his job through unemployment, sickness or retirement.[31] His solution was a comprehensive, basic insurance scheme based on workplace contributions by the male 'head of household' from which dependent spouses could also benefit.[32]

This started to unravel when, from the sixties onwards, married couples started separating in large numbers (leaving divorced wives with no eligibility for benefits), and single women without paid employment started to have children without husbands to support them. Although female workforce participation rates also began to rise in this period (so more women earned entitlements in their own right), career breaks for child-rearing and the popularity of part-time employment to fit in with family responsibilities inevitably meant that even working women often failed to accumulate strong contributions records.

Since the 1960s, the escalating divorce rate and the explosion in the number of single parent families has meant the welfare state has had to assume increasing financial responsibility for women with no claim on a husband's contributions, weak or non-existent contributions records of their own, and little or no pension entitlement when they reached retirement age. [33] This has resulted in an increasing reliance on means-tested benefits and the further marginalisation of the contributory principle.

Flat-rate benefits but graduated contributions

There has been one serious attempt since Beveridge to strengthen the insurance component of the benefits system, and this occurred when flat-rate contributions and benefits were replaced by earnings-related contributions and benefits in the 1960s. This change edged the UK closer to continental European social insurance schemes and was aimed at overcoming one of the key problems in the original Beveridge plan.

We have seen that benefits had to be kept low under Beveridge's scheme so the lowest-paid workers could afford the flat-rate contribution. The introduction of graduated payments and benefits allowed those who could afford it to pay more and to accumulate more benefits as a consequence. Low- and high-risk people still paid the same level of contributions (e.g. workers in insecure jobs paid no more than those in secure employment), so this was not like a commercial insurance system where different levels of premium reflect different levels of risk. But those on higher incomes could now get more generous benefits in return for higher weekly payments, and this helped narrow the gap between their income in work and the amount they received when they retired or became sick or unemployed.

Earnings-related contributions replaced the flat-rate National Insurance stamp in 1961. This coincided with the first attempt by government to offer graduated state retirement pensions in return for higher National Insurance payments. An 'earnings-related supplement' was introduced for unemployment and sickness benefits five years after that.[34]

Graduated benefits for the working-age population were short-lived, however. The earnings-related supplement was scrapped in 1982 as a government cost-saving measure and has never been reintroduced, although graduated contributions have continued to be levied ever since. Today, the more you earn, the more you pay, but you get nothing extra to show for it.

Graduated state pensions enjoyed a longer history. In 1961, workers whose employers had not contracted them out by offering an occupational pension scheme of their own were required to buy additional National Insurance 'units' which would buy a higher state pension on retirement. However, wary of the cost of this commitment, governments failed to up-rate the value of these units to keep pace with inflation. Between 1961 and 1975, the cost of living in Britain rose almost 300 per cent but the value of additional pension units did not change. Those who paid into the scheme were effectively defrauded.[35]

It was replaced in 1975 by the State Earnings Related Pension Scheme (SERPS), which in 2002 was revamped and rebranded as the 'Second State Pension'.[36] Under both of these later schemes, workers and their employers were required to pay an additional National Insurance contribution in return for an enhanced (and this time, inflation-proofed) state pension. As before, workers covered by a personal or occupational pension scheme could opt out, in which case they paid a lower National Insurance rate (this opt-out was eventually abolished in 2012 as a result of the 2007 Pension Act).

Once again, though, over time (and despite the promise of inflation-proofing), the value of the additional state pension was eroded. SERPS was watered down by reducing the accrual rate and by calculating entitlements on the basis of people's earnings averaged over their entire working life, rather than over their best 20 years of earnings.[37] The second state pension, which replaced it, reduced the earnings-related element, and in 2007 it was redesigned to evolve into a flat-rate payment over the next twenty or thirty years.[38]

As policy shifted away from providing a contributions-based top-up to the basic state pension, more emphasis was placed on providing means-tested supplements designed to concentrate help on the most needy pensioners.[39] Since 2003, this has been achieved mainly by the Pension Credit.

Under Pension Credit, retirees who have no private or occupational pension (and no other source of income), and/or whose National Insurance contributions do not qualify them for an enhanced state pension, nevertheless get their state pension increased to what is deemed an adequate level. Some 45 per cent of pensioners are eligible to claim Pension Credit, although one-third of them do not claim it.[40]

Pension Credit is driven entirely by need. That its introduction has completely undermined Beveridge's contributory principle, and the ethic of fairness on which it rests, can be seen if we compare the situation of two single pensioners, one with a complete National Insurance contributions record, and the other with no contributions at all.

In 2010, the first pensioner would have received the basic state pension of £95 per week. On top of that, he or she would have received either a private/occupational pension, or the second state pension. If the latter, they would have paid additional National Insurance contributions every week since 1975 to earn a right to the second state pension. Every penny they received in pension, they would have paid in for during their working life.

Now consider someone with no National Insurance

contributions record and no second pension. In 2010, they were eligible to claim a minimum guarantee of £130 per week in means-tested Pension Credit. None of this money had been covered by their own past contributions.[41] Yet this Pension Credit was worth £35 per week *more* than the first pensioner could get in their contributory basic state pension. To match it, the first pensioner had to pay enhanced contributions in order to receive a second state pension top-up.

Workers who during their working lives have been required to pay extra National Insurance contributions for a second state pension, or who have paid into a private or occupational scheme after opting out of the second state pension, might be excused for thinking they had been wasting their money. It turns out that non-contributory means-tested benefits like the Pension Credit would have topped them up anyway. By paying for their own enhanced pension, they have rendered themselves ineligible for this free top-up. To rub more salt into this wound, it is their taxes that are used to finance the non-contributory payments made to those who, unlike them, never contributed anything.

Of course, people who for whatever reason have made no financial contributions during their working lives have to be supported in their old age. But by paying them more-or-less the same as someone who has worked their whole life on low wages and has paid National Insurance contributions towards a basic state pension and a second state pension, the system clearly violates Haidt's principle of proportionality. Put simply, it seems grossly unfair.

Yet rather than rectifying this unfairness, reforms to the state pension system to be introduced in 2016 are going to reinforce it. The additional state pension is being scrapped altogether, bringing to an end the sorry fifty year history of graduated state pensions in Britain. In its place, the government will pay a new, higher 'basic' state pension to everyone who reaches retirement age with 35 years of National Insurance contributions to their name. This new, higher state pension will be paid at the equivalent of £144 per week in 2013 values.

But this is just £1.30 per week higher than the £142.70 to which someone on the full Pension Credit with no National Insurance contributions will be entitled.[42] Those who have paid in all their lives will therefore end up with one per cent more than those who have paid nothing at all.

There will be no opt-outs from this new state pension, so everyone (including people in occupational pension schemes and the self-employed) will in future have to pay the same (higher) rate of National Insurance. There will be no top-ups either, so everyone over retirement age will get the same amount from the government, provided they have paid full contributions for 35 years (or are deemed to have done so – see below).[43] As now, those who have paid contributions for longer than the maximum qualifying period will get nothing extra in their pension to show for it. Nor will the actual amount people have paid have any impact on the pension they receive – high earners will continue to pay more into the scheme than low earners (because National Insurance is levied as a percentage of pay) but will get the same state pension when they retire.[44]

Retired people with non-existent or inadequate contributions records will continue to qualify for means-tested assistance (the Pension Credit). This will bring their state retirement incomes up to the same level, give-or-take a pound or two, as the new basic pension paid to those who have a full National Insurance contributions record.[45] In this way, everyone will be guaranteed an adequate retirement income, irrespective of whether they have paid for it.

Most welfare economists seem to think this reform makes sense because it simplifies current arrangements.

Instead of some people getting a basic state pension plus a second state pension while others get a Pension Credit, everyone gets roughly the same amount. This makes the new system clearer and easier for everyone to understand so we should all be able to make better-informed decisions about our futures before we get to retirement age.

But the government does not only defend this reform on grounds of improved efficiency. It also says it will be 'fairer' than the present system.

The 2011 Green Paper claimed the new system will be 'fairer' because some women (as well as self-employed people) do not have a full second pension entitlement under current arrangements.[46] After 2016 they will be entitled to the new, enhanced basic pension. Meanwhile, employees (often men) with more than 35 years of contributions will get nothing extra for their efforts.[47] So while some get levelled up, others get levelled down.

This claim of enhanced 'fairness' was repeated in the 2013 White Paper. It says the new system will be 'fairer' because it will ensure that men and women get the same state pension, even though on average they have been earning different amounts while they are working, and they may have spent different amounts of time in the labour force (because women are more likely to take time out to raise children).[48]

The assumption on which these claims of greater fairness rest (but which is never explicitly spelled out or justified in the Green and White Papers) is that fairness is a matter of equalising outcomes rather than rewarding inputs.[49] The Director of the Institute of Fiscal Studies says our conception of fairness has changed since Beveridge, and that the new system reflects this: 'The new proposals encapsulate a different idea of fairness: that everyone is entitled to a basic income in retirement irrespective of contribution. The new system...ends any notion that what you get out should reflect what you put in.'[50]

But it is a curious notion of 'fairness' that holds that it is fair to give more money to those who have not paid in, and less to those who have. The result may be more equal, to be sure, but it is not obviously more fair. As we saw in Part I, most people in Britain think fairness is about just desserts, not equal outcomes.

The White Paper's claim that the new system will be fairer to women who spend time out of the workforce ignores the fact that we all have some fifty years of potential working life between the minimum school-leaving age and the age at which we may claim a state pension. Given we need only accumulate 35 years of contributions in that time to qualify for a full state pension, this allows everyone up to 15 years out of the labour force to continue their education and/or to raise children. Men and women alike therefore enjoy ample opportunity over a lifetime to accumulate the minimum contributions record required to qualify for a full pension. So why is it now considered fairer to give everyone the same amount regardless of whether they choose to exploit this opportunity?

In the move to the new pension system, these arguments about fairness seem never to have been seriously aired or considered. It has simply been taken for-granted that equal outcomes for all is the fairest way to organise things. As a result, this reform has effectively killed off the contributory principle as it applies to the funding of state retirement incomes.[51] In the future, everyone over retirement age will be given a basic income by the state, irrespective of whether they have paid National Insurance contributions, how much they have paid, or for how long. As we shall see, this collapse of the contributory principle has left many experts wondering why we are bothering to keep National Insurance contributions at all.

The increasingly blurred distinction between contributory and tax-funded benefits

At the same time as graduated benefits have been disappearing, the sharp distinction between insured and uninsured benefits has also been blurring.

In 1996, a new Jobseeker's Allowance (JSA) replaced both (insured) Unemployment Benefit and (uninsured) income support for the unemployed. Although the contributory principle was notionally carried forward in the continuing distinction between 'contribution-based' and 'income-based' JSA, there was actually little difference between the two from a claimant's point of view, and many people have been left bewildered by the distinction.[52]

The contributions-based JSA is worth the same as the income-based allowance. It only lasts for six months, and the same activity conditions and sanctions can be applied to both. One difference is that contribution-based JSA is not means-tested on household income (which could be important if a partner is earning) or on a claimant's capital and savings. But claimants can still have some or all of it withdrawn if they have an income from a pension or part-time earnings of their own.[53]

Another difference, which works *against* those with a contributions record, is that income-based JSA automatically entitles recipients to a range of other welfare benefits including free prescriptions, free school meals, maximum housing benefit, maximum council tax benefit, and the possibility of one-off payments from the Social Fund. Unemployed people with National Insurance contributions enjoy no such automatic entitlements.[54]

This blurring of the distinction between insured unemployment benefit (contribution-based JSA) and the uninsured equivalent (income-based JSA) is mirrored in the rules governing the Employment and Support Allowance, which replaced Incapacity Benefit in 2008. Here too, there is a distinction between 'contribution-based' and 'income-based' claims, but as with JSA, the value of the benefit is the same for both, and those without a contributions record qualify automatically for other benefits which those with contributions may not get.

For most JSA and ESA claimants, therefore, it makes precious little material difference whether or not they have paid National Insurance contributions, and some claimants with a record of contributions may actually find themselves disadvantaged as a result. Clearly, the contributory principle has been fatally undermined by these developments. [55] Britain today is one of a very few OECD countries where claimants with no record of work-based contributions receive the same value of cash benefits as those who have built up insurance entitlements.[56] The Labour Party has recently recognised this inequity and is currently considering how people with long contributions records might be credited with higher benefits.[57]

The introduction of tax credits in the Blair years further undermined the point of contributory benefits. Despite their name, tax credits are means-tested benefits financed out of general taxation – welfare payments masquerading under another name. [58] They were introduced as an anti-poverty measure, for they boost the incomes of low-paid workers (as well as jobless families on welfare), thereby helping to push them above the government's 'poverty line'.

Like all means-tested benefits for working-age people, tax credits discourage work by penalising those who start to earn a bit more each week (because the benefit is withdrawn as earnings rise). To reduce this disincentive effect, a long 'income taper' was created so that eligibility for benefits declines gradually, rather than being sharply withdrawn. But this means that people earning quite high wages can still be eligible for a tax credit. Around six million adults (including nine out of ten families with children) currently qualify for this hand-out, and they include households with above-median incomes.[59]

The expansion of tax credits has severely skewed the benefits system away from Beveridge's vision of a contributory system with a supplementary, means-tested safety net, towards a largely tax-funded, needs-based system with little or no room for personal responsibility. In 1990, 37 per cent of the cash benefits claimed by working-age families were contributory and 63 per cent non-contributory; by 2010, the share of contributory benefits had shrunk to 26 per cent, with non-contributory benefits accounting for 74 per cent.[60] In 2011-12, the government spent £95bn on working-age benefits, of which £22bn went on tax credits, and only £10bn consisted of contributory benefits.[61]

All of these non-contributory benefits (income-based JSA, income-related ESA, child tax credits and working tax credits) are in turn now being replaced by a new single benefit, the 'Universal Credit', which is being phased in between 2013 and 2017.[62] This new benefit also replaces Income Support and Housing Benefit. Contributory JSA and ESA will continue (at least for now), but Universal Credit is set to become the principal component of our welfare system. Like the various benefits it is replacing, it is means-tested and tax-financed. If you can demonstrate need, you will qualify for it, and the greater your need, the more you will get.[63] Past contributions will be wholly irrelevant.

Pretending people have made contributions when they haven't

The definition of a 'contribution' has also been diluted and confused so much over the last 40 years that it has almost ceased to have any significant meaning. When Beveridge set the National Insurance system up, eligibility for benefits was determined simply by whether you had paid sufficient stamps over a given period. But in 1975, new regulations allowed various categories of people to claim National Insurance 'credits' for time spent on 'acceptable' activities other than paid work. This meant they could qualify for a full state pension, even with an incomplete work record.

The unemployed, those claiming carer's allowance, women receiving maternity pay, young workers under 18, workers over 60 and those in full-time training courses can nowadays all claim National Insurance credits, even if they are not working and/or not actually making any National Insurance contributions. In addition, since 1979, parents looking after young children at home have been able to offset their child-rearing years against the number of years of contributions required to qualify for a full pension (so-called 'Home Responsibilities Protection'), and in 2010, they too were allowed to claim National Insurance contribution credits for time spent out of the labour force looking after their children.[64] Workers earning between £102 and £139 per week are also treated as having paid National Insurance contributions, even though they are exempt.[65]

As a result of these concessions, most adults nowadays qualify for the state pension on the strength of their 'contributions', even though many have in reality paid little or nothing. The government estimates that about 90 per cent of retired people will qualify for the new basic pension – far more than will have paid 35 years of National Insurance contributions.[66]

It is easy to understand why these concessions have been made over the years, for as we saw earlier, social and economic changes since Beveridge (notably the casualisation of work and the dramatic changes affecting family life) have left increasing numbers of people without a right to the contribution-based state retirement pension. But pretending that people have paid contributions, when in reality they have not, has made a mockery of Beveridge's original contributory principle. As one review concludes: 'A social insurance programme which [gives] benefit entitlements to those who are credited with "fictitious" contribution rights without having actually made monetary contributions is in danger of losing legitimacy in the eyes of actual contributors.'[67]

It is also clearly unfair on those who have worked and paid real contributions through their lives to give the same entitlements to those who have made no contributions – although few commentators seem to have the gumption to say this.[68]

Turning Beveridge upside down

The UK social security system today has clearly drifted well away from the contributory principle and is based almost entirely on demonstration of 'need'. This long-term shift has been driven by parties on both sides of politics.

Left-wing governments have wanted to reduce poverty by raising the value of non-contributory benefits and extending National Insurance cover to groups with little or no contribution history. Right-wing governments have wanted to limit escalating state spending by increasing means-testing of welfare so as to target benefits on those who need them most. In both cases, the result has been to erode the contributory principle in favour of tax-funded, means-tested welfare.[69]

People who have made no contribution to the National Insurance fund are nowadays commonly treated as if they had. Those who have accumulated earned entitlements find they confer very little advantage over those who have paid little or nothing. Unemployment, sickness and family benefits (including tax credits) are paid to working-age people regardless of their National Insurance contributions, and the new Universal Credit places means-tested, tax-funded benefits at the heart of the welfare system. For retirees, the second state pension financed by additional National Insurance contributions has been rendered meaningless by the non-contributory Pension Credit, and in future, everybody will get almost the same retirement income from the government, irrespective of whether or not they have paid for it.

In 1948, when Beveridge's reforms were first introduced, more than 60 per cent of social security spending went on contributory benefits, and just 13 per cent went on means-tested benefits.[70] Today, just 41 per cent goes on contributory benefits, and the figure is only this high because the state pension absorbs such a large proportion of all social security spending.[71] Take out the state pension, and less than 10 per cent of all the benefits paid out each year are contributory.[72]

We saw earlier that Beveridge wanted to make contributory insurance the core of Britain's welfare system, and to residualise means-tested welfare. Seventy years later, we have achieved precisely the opposite.

Should we scrap National Insurance?

Many commentators now argue with some justification that National Insurance contributions have ceased to have any substantial significance and are better understood simply as another form of income tax. This being the case, they say, it would make more sense to absorb National Insurance payments into the income tax system so that workers pay only one tax on their wages and employers have only one deduction to process.

National insurance receipts account for 20 per cent of all government revenue each year,[73] although many of us are unaware of quite how much we are paying. Revenue from NICs exceeds that from VAT and is two-thirds of the amount raised from income tax.[74] In the 2012/13 tax year, employees making Class I contributions were paying 12 per cent on weekly earnings between £146 and £817, and two per cent on earnings above that. But their employers were also paying 13.8 per cent on all their workers' earnings above £146. Economists point out that, in the end, the cost of this also falls on employees, for the hefty employers' contribution depresses the wages paid to workers.[75] Effectively, therefore, workers who may only be paying a 20 per cent rate of income tax are also paying a 25.8 per cent additional levy on their earnings in the form of employer and employee NICs.

Many employees are unaware of the full extent of the deductions being levied on their earnings.[76] Many basic rate taxpayers would be astounded and appalled if they realised that they are paying what are effectively two income tax levies amounting to a total marginal rate of 45.8 per cent.

Focus group research commissioned by the government in the late nineties found that many people think of their National Insurance contributions (quite wrongly) 'as a personal kitty'.[77] They do not even think of their own NICs as a tax on their incomes, and it never occurs to them that their employers' NICs are also bearing down on their wages. To many people, National Insurance feels like compulsory saving, which is why there is a greater willingness to pay NICs than to pay income tax.[78] This naiveté has been exploited by politicians down the years, not least when the Blair government promised at the 2001 election not to raise income tax rates but then hiked NICs instead as soon as it was returned to power.[79]

The influential Institute of Fiscal Studies (IFS) is in the

forefront of the campaign to roll NICs into the tax system, and like many other critics, it points to this opaqueness as one of the key reasons for such a reform. It suggests that National Insurance is a tax by another name, but it lacks the transparency which we should demand of any taxes. Not only are many of us unaware of its impact on our pockets, directly (through our own NICs) and indirectly (through those of our employers), but many of us have little idea what our National Insurance entitlements are, or what our contributions are buying. When asked what their contributions pay for, more people mention the NHS than pensions, but the NHS is mainly funded out of general taxation and there is no link between the NICs people pay and their entitlement to NHS treatment.[80]

Critics like the IFS point out that National Insurance is not genuine 'insurance', and that the link between contributions paid and benefits received is 'vanishingly weak'.[81] National Insurance is a second layer of income tax, but unlike income tax itself, it is regressive (for although contributions are based on a percentage of earnings, the marginal rate drops to just two per cent beyond the £817 weekly ceiling). Collection of NICs also creates unnecessary complexity for employers and adds to business costs: in addition to paying the employer's contribution, businesses have to calculate and process two different sets of deductions when calculating employees' pay.[82] This is particularly burdensome for small employers.[83] Running two different systems also costs the government about £300m each year in additional administration costs.[84]

For thirty years, the IFS has been arguing that the National Insurance system should be wound up. In its submission to a 1984 government review of social security, it spelt out the standard economists' argument that the primary goal of social security is to prevent poverty, and that this is best achieved by targeting benefits according to need. It calculated then that 26 per cent of government spending on pensions, and 45 per cent of sickness and unemployment benefits, were being 'wasted' on people who were not 'poor' but who nevertheless qualified for payments because of their NIC records. Better, said the IFS, to limit these benefits to those whose incomes fell below a specified minimum level and to stop worrying about past National Insurance contributions.[85]

Thirty years later, the IFS is still arguing much the same line.[86] It says many people who need benefits are excluded due to weak or non-existent contributions records, yet many other people who do not need support get it because they have established an entitlement through their contributions. The answer is to collapse National Insurance into the income tax system: 'We need to move away from having separate systems of income tax and NICs, with different sets of rules and exemptions, pointlessly increasing administration and compliance costs and making the system less transparent. National Insurance is not a true social insurance scheme: it is just another tax on earnings... The two systems need to be merged.'[87]

The IFS claims there is 'a widespread consensus outside government that such a merger would be desirable in principle.'[88] This certainly seems to be true of business interests and many pro-market think tanks.

♦ A 2006 survey of businesses by the Tax Reform Commission found 65 per cent supported a full merger of National Insurance and income tax.[89] A 2012 survey of members of the Institute of Directors found 79 per cent favoured a merger with only 11 per cent opposed.[90]

♦ A 2012 joint report by the Taxpayers' Alliance and the Institute of Directors claims that scrapping National Insurance would stimulate economic growth and make tax on earnings much more transparent. It argues for abolition of both employers' and employees' NICs and their replacement by a 36 per cent basic income tax rate, falling to 30 per cent by 2020.[91]

◆ The pro-free market Reform think tank argues that the separate National Insurance system creates more costs for employers and unnecessary complexity. It reasons that, since the 2016 pension reform will give everyone more-or-less the same income regardless of their NIC history, the contributory principle should be scrapped and the state pension means-tested so it concentrates on those who really need help.[92]

◆ The Conservative-leaning Centre for Policy Studies says the introduction of the Universal Credit and the new basic pension has finally undermined the contributory principle. This is 'a cause for regret', but National Insurance should now be scrapped. The state pension should be based on years of residency and financed out of general taxation, and unemployment, sickness and maternity benefits for workers should be financed by a Payroll Tax to replace employer NICs.[93]

These arguments for scrapping National Insurance seem compelling, and when the present Coalition government came into office, there were confident reports in the media that the Chancellor was preparing to listen to the experts and do away with it.[94] But it hasn't happened.

Instead, in his 2011 Budget speech, George Osborne announced he was consulting on a merger of the operation of income tax and NICs (e.g. by aligning thresholds and time periods). But he stopped short of advocating abolition. Indeed, he pointed to the 'long-established principle in

Britain that if you work and you make contributions... you are making a contribution to your future pension, and I think a government should think long and hard before it abolished that.'[95]

The real reason for this backtracking seems to have had less to do with 'principle' than with an attack of political jitters. Given that the government is happy to pay the same pension to people who have contributed as to those who have not, the Chancellor's expressed regard for the 'long-established principle' of contributory benefits can probably be taken with a pinch of salt. The reason neither he nor any other political leader wants to scrap National Insurance is more likely that the basic rate of income tax would have to rise substantially just to replace the 12 per cent now paid in employee NICs, and by a huge amount if employer NICs were also rolled into income tax. This could prove politically toxic.

The problem is largely one of appearances. Most basic rate taxpayers would not notice any difference in their take-home pay if employee NICs were combined with income tax, and employer contributions could be replaced with a Payroll Tax to avoid adding them to people's income tax bills.[96] But no government wants to be associated with hiking the basic income tax rate from 20 per cent to 32 per cent in one leap, and even the IFS recognises that this could prove 'politically suicidal'.[97]

Dissolving National Insurance into income tax would also involve some difficult adjustments which would inevitably create some angry and very vociferous losers.[98] The self-employed and members of occupational pension schemes are already seeing their reduced National Insurance rate raised to the full 12 per cent with the change to the new basic pension. Investors and savers, who currently pay income tax but no NICs on their dividends and interest payments, would see deductions from their incomes rise by a thumping 12 per cent. So would employees under the age of 16 or over retirement age, for they too are currently exempt from NICs, but they do pay income tax.

Winners would include people with several jobs (for NICs are assessed separately for each employment while income tax is levied on total earnings from all work), and those with lumpy earnings profiles (for NICs are assessed weekly while income tax is averaged across a whole year's earnings). But when it comes to electoral arithmetic, every politician knows that losers make a lot more noise than winners.

A means-tested basic pension

The corrosion of our social insurance system should never have been allowed to happen. Ideally, we should have retained and nurtured a welfare system based primarily on the principle of contributions. As the corny old Irish joke has it, the best way to get to where we want to go would be to start from somewhere other than where we now find ourselves.

But we cannot re-wind history. And we should not keep shaking up the system either. Both the retirement pension and working-age benefits have recently been subject to a series of radical reforms and upheavals which it is neither practical nor desirable to start unpicking now.

Many working-age benefits are being reorganised into a single Universal Credit, and the state pension and second pension are being combined into a new, enhanced, basic pension. These are major transformations which cannot sensibly be re-thought at this late stage. The key question, therefore, is how to build on the system that we now have in such a way that the contributory principle is not lost (as seems all too likely at the moment) but is, where possible, restored and strengthened.

Pension reform is the key, for the state pension lies at the heart of the NI system. Of the £70bn paid out by the National Insurance Fund in 2008-09, £61bn (87 per cent) was for pensions (£7bn went on incapacity benefits, and just £700m on contribution-based JSA).[99] Any strategy aimed at strengthening the contributory principle has to include the funding of retirement pensions.

We have seen that, with the latest reforms to the pension system, the contributory principle has been all but lost. People are deemed to have made contributions even when they haven't, and the full means-tested payments available to those with a weak or non-existent contributions record will be little different from the pension payable to those who have paid in for the full 35 years. Commentators at the IFS and elsewhere are right – there is not much point any longer in retaining the distinction between the contributory state pension and the non-contributory Pension Credit guarantee. It has become meaningless, and we should let it go.

What this means is that, reluctantly, we have to go along with the critics who say we should phase out what remains of the contributory state pension and fund the new basic state pension out of general taxation. Anyone who can pass a residency test (say, a minimum of ten years' UK residence) would then be eligible for the pension, irrespective of their work history, and the Pension Credit could be scrapped. The 12 per cent Class I employee National Insurance contribution could be folded into the basic income tax rate, as proposed by the IFS and others in the reports reviewed above, and employer contributions could be transformed into a simple Payroll Tax.

But there is an important corollary. If the new state pension is to be made available to everyone who has fulfilled UK residency criteria, irrespective of their past financial contributions, then there is a compelling argument for means-testing it on household income. Either we have a contribution-based pension, like the social insurance systems in many continental European countries, or we have a means-tested pension funded out of general taxation, as they do in Australia.[100] The danger is that we seem to be drifting into a cross between the two, a non-means-tested yet increasingly non-contributory universal pension which combines the worst of both worlds, offering neither the fairness of a contributory scheme nor the efficiency savings of a means-tested one.

Once the contributory principle goes, taxpayers will be picking up the tab for all state pensions. But when tax revenues (rather than individual contributions) are the source of funding, there is no longer any justification for giving a state pension to people who do not really need it. If we have to accept that the days of the contributory state pension are behind us, we must also recognise that Beveridge's vision of a non-means-tested, flat-rate pension has to go as well.

Those who have already built-up National Insurance contributions should, of course, have these honoured when they retire, irrespective of their financial circumstances at that time. These entitlements could be frozen (as a percentage of the inflation-adjusted value of the current state pension) and paid when people reach retirement age; or bonds could be credited to people's personal pension funds to the value of their current entitlements, maturing on retirement when they could be put towards the purchase of an annuity.[101]

Whichever way existing entitlements are safeguarded, from a specified change-over date, workers would cease to pay any more NICs and would therefore cease to build up any more state pension entitlements. The result, over time, is that a substantial number of retirees who under the existing system would qualify for a full state pension would no longer be eligible for it because they or their partners have income from other sources (including occupational and private pensions) which takes the household above the means test limit.[102]

The major advantage of a change to a means-tested state pension is, of course, that over time it would save money – lots of it. We saw earlier that the IFS estimated in 1984 that 26 per cent of the money spent on UK state pensions is 'wasted' on people who do not need any additional support from the government. A means test that prevented this money being spent would end up saving up to £20bn every year.

The actual savings could be a lot higher than this, given the likely impact of the new, auto-enrolled 'workplace pensions' on levels of retirement saving. As we shall see in Part III, almost all workers will in future be enrolled by their employers in a private pension scheme funded jointly with their employer, and this could mean that, in years to come, many more people will retire with an occupational or private pension big enough to reduce or eliminate their claim to a means-tested state pension. In Australia, where the means-tested state pension runs alongside compulsory participation in an occupational scheme, only 55 per cent of retirees qualify for the full state pension, and by the middle of this century, this will be down to just over one-third.[103] If this pattern were replicated in Britain, the expenditure savings from means-testing could eventually approach £40bn or more each year at today's values.

These savings will only accrue gradually, however, because it will take many years for all the people with existing National Insurance entitlements to pass through the system. But as claims based on the old system of NICs gradually decline, the cost to the government of pension payments would start to fall relative to what it would have been under existing arrangements. Each year, expenditure on state pensions would reduce a little further.

Another advantage of a change like this is that it would end the arbitrary system of awarding selected groups of people with National Insurance credits, even when they haven't paid anything. At the moment, some favoured groups – parents raising their children at home, people caring for elderly relatives, part-timers who earn below the NI threshold, unemployed workers, women on maternity leave – are selected by government for special treatment by pretending they have made National Insurance contributions. This creates unfairness, for not only are people who have paid contributions treated no differently from those who have not, but some non-contributors are given credits while others are not.

Under the new system, there would be no scope for this sort of arbitrary political patronage. Parents, carers and other currently-favoured groups would be eligible to apply for the means-tested basic pension in the same way as everybody else. If they don't get one, it will not be because they haven't accumulated the required contributions record, but because they have sufficient income from other sources such that they don't need one. The unfairness inherent in arbitrarily treating some groups in the population differently from others would be overcome.

So what happened to the fairness principle?

Ending the arbitrary system of National Insurance credits would promote fairness, but looking at the wider picture, scrapping the contributory state pension and moving everyone to a means-tested one threatens to leave us with an even less fair system than we have at the moment.

Two (linked) injustices stand out. One is that workers who save for a private or workplace pension will get penalised by losing some or all of their state pension. The other is that the younger generation of workers will be expected to pay the state pensions of existing retirees, even though they may not get a state pension themselves when they reach retirement age.

The first of these injustices is inherent to any means-tested benefit, for when we target payments at those who cannot provide for themselves, we inevitably penalise the thrifty and discourage self-reliance. It poses a major problem, for why would workers bother saving in a private or occupational pension scheme (or investing in other assets that will generate a flow of income in retirement), if they know this will render them ineligible for a taxpayer-funded state pension?

To prevent people from deliberately running down their savings to make themselves eligible for a state pension (the 'moral hazard' problem), it would almost certainly be necessary to force workers to set aside a portion of their earnings in a personal retirement plan (as Australia did when it set up its compulsory superannuation system in 1992).[104] As we shall see in Part III, participation in the new workplace pensions is not compulsory at the moment (people can opt out), but if we start to means-test state pensions, it will probably need to be.

This doesn't resolve the fairness problem, of course, although it does make a means-tested pension workable. It means that one section of the population will work all their lives, pay taxes and build up their own retirement savings, only to render themselves ineligible for a means-tested state pension. Meanwhile, another group which (for whatever reason) has not been economically active reaches retirement with few or no assets, yet qualifies for a full state pension funded by taxpayers. The fact that our existing system already contains elements of this unfairness (we have seen that those with no NICs will end up getting almost as much in Pension Credit as those with a lifetime of contributions will get in the new basic state pension) does not make it any more palatable.

The second injustice is that means-testing the state pension involves a transfer of wealth between generations. If NICs are scrapped, future generations will still pay the same amount from their wage packets as the current generation of workers does (the new basic rate of income tax would incorporate the current basic tax rate of 20 per cent, plus the current employee NI contribution of 12 per cent). However, with a means test, the 12 per cent component will no longer automatically qualify them for a state pension. As a generation, they will pay the same as their parents did into the system, but will get less out. They will be the squeezed generation.

Given that this generation is already saddled with repaying a record level of National Debt, is carrying higher levels of personal debt (partly as a result of changes to the financing of higher education), is having to pay higher real prices for its housing, and is having to work for longer than those who are now entering retirement, it hardly seems fair to saddle them with yet another burden.[105] The trouble is, some generational inequity (or what one analyst calls a 'limited government default') is inevitable if we ever want to get away from our increasingly unsustainable pay-as-you-go state pension scheme.[106] This is a move which becomes more pressing, the longer we put it off.

We saw earlier that a generational game of pass-the-parcel started when the post-war Attlee government decided to pay full pensions to existing retirees who had not contributed towards them. These pensions were funded out of the contributions of existing workers. Ever since then, each generation of workers has had to pay for the previous generation's pensions. As average life expectancy has risen, and birth rates have fallen, this arrangement has become increasingly expensive and unsustainable.

Government spending on the state pension and associated benefits is projected to rise from 5.7 per cent of GDP in 2010-11 to 6.9 per cent in 2050-51. A 21 per cent rise over 40 years may not sound like an unmanageable increase, but this assumes that GDP keeps growing steadily over the next few decades. In real money terms (expressed in 2012 prices), the cost of state pensions will rise from £84bn to £250bn over this forty-year period.[107] This has led the Organisation for Economic Co-operation and Development to warn the UK government that if it fails to cut the spiralling cost of our ageing population, both the state pension and health systems in Britain could collapse.[108]

These figures suggest we have reached the point where something has to change. Inevitably, when the music does eventually stop, the generation left holding the parcel will have to pay for the pensions of those who are already retired as well as putting money aside for its own retirement.

Freezing contribution entitlements and then means-testing the state pension is probably the least onerous solution to this problem, for it only entails a partial loss of entitlements (those who still need support will continue to get the means-tested pension), and this loss will gradually be offset (to some extent) by consequent tax savings.

During the long transition period, workers reaching retirement age each year will on average have slightly less entitlement to a state pension than those retiring the year before (because they will have accumulated fewer NICs). Those with private pensions or other sources of income which exclude them from the new means-tested state pension will therefore receive slightly less in their state pension than the cohort in front of them. But as expenditure savings accumulate from the means-testing of these new retirees, they can gradually be passed back as tax cuts which will enable those behind them to contribute more to their own pension pots.[109]

The burden of the transition will obviously be easier if the economy continues to grow steadily over the long term. Annual growth of three per cent would double average real incomes in forty years – the span of an ordinary working lifetime. Inter-generational transfer of housing wealth may also help offset the next generation's reduced state pension entitlements. The baby boomers are the first generation in British history where a majority own their own homes.[110] Their children will therefore be the first generation of mass inheritors of housing wealth, even if some boomers squander their money rather than bequeathing it, and others use it up paying for nursing home expenses. Many should therefore be able to use their legacies to help fund their retirements.[111]

The key point to understand, though, is that the burden of financing their parents' retirement already exists for this generation of workers. It is not as if they have a choice. Whether or not the state pension is reformed, this liability has already been incurred (even though government accounts often fail to make it explicit). As Nicholas Barr observes: 'Once the gift to the first generation under a PAYG scheme has been made, there is a cost that future generations cannot escape.'[112]

The question, therefore, is not whether the current generation of workers should be required to pay the state pension entitlements built up by its parents; it is whether this generation should pass the ballooning pension debt down the line for its children to deal with, as previous generations have done. The state pension entitlements of their parents are a 'sunk cost' which they can do nothing to change.[113]

We started this discussion of the future of our National Insurance system by insisting that the fairness principle – what Haidt calls the principle of proportionality – must underpin any reform. Yet we now appear to have ended up accepting the case for scrapping the contributory state pension and moving to a means-tested pension which entails a double unfairness. It is unfair on those who are working and paying taxes, for they will have to fund a pension for other people which they may not get themselves, and it is unfair on the younger generation of workers, for they will have to pay for universal pensions for their parents while accepting means-tested pensions for themselves. In Part III, we shall consider how the fairness principle might be rescued from this wreckage.

PART III

Rescuing the Contributory Principle

The modern welfare state is designed to do two things. First, it supports those who cannot support themselves at any given time by transferring resources from relatively richer to relatively poorer households (the inter-personal *income redistribution* function). The richest fifth of households do most of the heavy lifting – in 2010/11, they paid on average £20,125 more in taxes than they received in benefits and welfare state services. The poorest fifth, by contrast, received on average £10,153 more than they paid. Slightly more than half of all households (53 per cent) were net beneficiaries of tax/welfare redistribution.[1]

Second, the welfare state also helps people 'level out' their incomes over their own lifetimes (the intra-personal *income smoothing* function). It does this by taking resources from them when they are earning and/or have few financial responsibilities, and giving them back (as a cash income or services in kind) at times when they are not earning (e.g. as a result of sickness, unemployment or retirement) and/or the demands on their budgets are greater (e.g. when they are raising children).

In Britain, inter-personal income redistribution is achieved mainly through the use of 'progressive' taxation and payment of cash benefits. Intra-personal income smoothing is achieved more by provision of universal services, such as schooling, health care and personal social services (although parts of the benefits system – notably the state pension – also make a significant contribution to income smoothing). Because most of us pay towards the cost of these services at various points in our lives, and most of us make at least some use of them before we die, they tend to have quite a limited impact on the distribution of resources between households, and in some cases – such as higher education – their net redistributive effect may even be negative (i.e. richer households gain more from them than poorer ones do).

What role does National Insurance play in all this? We saw in Part II that Beveridge never intended the National Insurance system to be redistributive between richer and poorer households. Rather, it was designed simply to reallocate earnings across people's life spans. In return for a flat-rate weekly contribution (the same amount for everyone, rich or poor), workers were guaranteed a flat-rate, basic income in retirement and at times during their working lives when they could not earn a living.

This changed from the 1960s onwards, when National Insurance contributions were linked to people's incomes by moving to a percentage levy (the more you earn, the more you pay). Even so, National Insurance is still not levied 'progressively' like income tax, and the marginal percentage levied on employees actually falls once their earnings rise beyond the 'upper earnings limit'.[2] Like the universal welfare services, therefore, National Insurance contributes more to income smoothing than to income redistribution.

Paying our own benefits:
simultaneous tax/welfare churning

Given that the welfare state has this two-fold function, reallocating resources vertically at any one time between richer and poorer households and horizontally over an extended period of time between different life stages of the same households, the obvious question is how much of the total budget goes on income redistribution, and how much on income smoothing?

Table 1 provides part of the answer. This divides the UK population in 2010-11 into five equally-sized income groups, based on people's reported 'original incomes' (i.e. the money they have coming in before the state gives them cash or services and takes taxes off them), adjusting for differences in household size and composition.[3] People are then ranked according to these original incomes from poorest ('Quintile 1') to richest ('Quintile 5').

The table traces the impact on the income of each of these quintiles of the cash welfare benefits they receive, the direct and indirect tax payments they make, and the value of government services in kind (like 'free' health and education) they consume. By comparing the total value of all the social provisions they receive from the government with the total value of all the taxes they pay to it, we can gauge the extent to which the welfare state at any one point in time is redistributing money between people as against 'churning' their own money back to them.

Comparing first the figures for 'original income' and 'final income', it is clear that significant redistribution from rich to poor is occurring. A ratio of 16:1 between the original incomes of the lowest and highest quintiles (£5,089:£81,501) is reduced to just 4:1 on final incomes (£15,242:£61,376). The poorest fifth of households on average raise their annual income by a factor of three (from just over £5,000 to more than £15,000) as a result of government taxes and spending, and the people in the next group up improve their incomes twofold. At the other end of the scale, the richest fifth of households see their final incomes fall on average by a quarter (from just over 80 to just over 60 thousand pounds).

Table 1: Income, taxes and benefits by quintile groups, 2010/11[4]

	Quintile groups:				
	Bottom	*2nd*	*3rd*	*4th*	*Top*
Original income	5,089	11,764	22,482	39,642	81,501
Cash benefits	7,040	8,322	6,655	4,098	2,115
Benefits in kind	7,749	7,584	7,459	6,825	5,826
Direct tax & NICs	1,271	2,510	4,755	9,002	19,727
Indirect taxes	3,365	3,741	4,770	6,033	8,339
Final income	15,242	21,419	27,071	35,529	61,376

In the middle of the distribution, inevitably, the net impact of government activity is much less marked. Members of the third quintile end up slightly better off, and those in the fourth quintile slightly worse off, as a result of the government's efforts, but the impact is not very great in either case. Put another way, churning is at its height for middle-income households who take out more-or-less what they put in.

What is most striking about Table 1, however, is what it reveals about the extent of tax/welfare 'churning' in all income quintiles. Even in the poorest group, where each person receives an average of £14,789 in assistance from the state, they still pay an average of £4,636 in taxes. For every £1 the poorest people receive in benefits or services, they contribute 31p of their own money. At the other end of the distribution, the most affluent earners pay an average annual tax bill of £28,066, but they receive back 28 per cent of it (£7,941) in benefits and services. For those around the middle of the distribution, receipts and payments more-or-less balance out.

Table 1 confirms that the redistribution function of the welfare state is achieved mainly by cash benefits and progressive income taxes. The bottom two quintiles receive cash benefits worth almost four times as much as those going to the top quintile, but the value of the services in kind they receive differs much less, the richest group receiving almost £6,000 worth of services, in comparison with less than £8,000 going to the poorest group. As for the taxes they pay, the richest group pays 15 times more income tax and NICs than the poorest, but only two-and-a-half times more indirect tax. It seems from these figures that tax/welfare churning is driven mainly by the state's provision of universal services like health and education, and by indirect taxes such as VAT and duties on alcohol and tobacco.

Lifetime churning (or what Tony Hancock can teach us about the welfare state)

This, however, is only part of the story, for in reality, tax/welfare churning is much more extensive than Table 1 suggests. Table 1 represents a single snapshot at just one point, frozen in time, but over the course of their lives, people move between income quintiles as their circumstances change.

The people in the higher income quintiles, for example, are nearly all working (fewer than one in ten are retired). This is not surprising, for you are unlikely to appear among the highest-income households if you have no earnings. Many of those in the lower quintiles, by contrast, are not working: one-third of those in the two poorest groups are retired; many others are jobless and living on benefits. Again, this is not surprising, for living on a pension or on welfare with no other earnings, you are likely to find yourself towards the bottom of the income distribution.

Move the picture forward, however, and like the crystals in a kaleidoscope, people start changing places. Those who found themselves in the bottom income group because they were temporarily sick or unemployed get back into jobs and move into higher income groups. Well-paid working women leave employment to have children and see their incomes fall, and other women whose children are growing up rejoin the labour force and see their incomes rise. Students on low incomes complete their studies and find well-remunerated employment. Older workers who were on the top of the pay scale retire and take a big drop in income. Some couples divorce and become poorer; others see their kids leave home and become richer. Overall, the amount of movement taking place across the income distribution as people pass through different stages of their lives is substantial.

One of the most important (and at the time, astonishing) findings of recent social scientific research in Britain has been the discovery of an extensive turnover in the composition of different income groups, even over quite small periods of time. Researchers used to assume when discussing 'poverty', for example, that they were dealing with more-or-less the same groups of people from one year to the next. We now know that this is not the case, for the composition of those below the 'poverty line' keeps changing.

The British Household Panel Study follows the same sample of people, re-interviewing them every year. It reports that half of those in the poorest tenth of the population in one year are no longer in the poorest tenth the following year. Although some do 'fall back' into this bottom income group in later periods, the study looked at the period from 1991 to 2001 and found that only four in ten of those in the poorest decile in 1991 were also there in 2001. Fully one quarter of them had moved into the top half of the income distribution. Of the 18 per cent of households below the 'poverty line' in 1991, only two per cent remained there for each of the next ten years.[5]

The implications of all this income shifting for our understanding of the relative importance of redistribution and churning in the welfare state are huge, for it means that many of those who are classified in Table 1 as receiving significant net payments from the government will at another time be net contributors, and vice versa. Churning, in other words, is likely to be much more extensive than this table suggests once we take account of the changes that people experience in the course of their lifetimes.

In a work of major significance, John Hills and his team attempted some years ago to estimate the total taxes paid, and total value of welfare services received, by different income groups over the course of their entire lives. Although the analysis itself is now quite dated, the patterns it revealed in the early 1990s are probably broadly similar today. (Research updating Hills's work is ongoing at the time of writing.)[6]

Hills divided the population into income deciles based on people's estimated, equivalised earnings over a whole lifetime.[7] He then calculated how much on average the people in each decile will pay into the welfare system in tax over a full lifetime, and how much they will get back from government spending on social security, education and the NHS (but excluding housing subsidies and personal social services). The analysis assumed that tax rates and welfare entitlements remained the same as they were at the time of the study in 1991.

His results confirmed that the British welfare state

operates much more as a system of intra-personal income smoothing than as a mechanism of inter-personal income redistribution. The results (based on the 1991 tax and welfare system, but with money values updated to 2001 prices) are summarised in Figure 1.

Fig.1: The self-financing of welfare benefits over a lifetime by different lifetime income deciles[8]

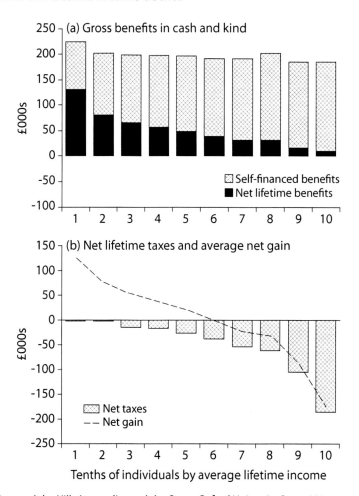

Source: John Hills, Inequality and the State, Oxford University Press, 2004

Looking first at the top diagram, Fig.1a ('Gross benefits in cash and kind'), the first point to note is that lifetime withdrawals from the welfare state (given by the height of each of the bars) are remarkably even over all income groups. The very lowest lifetime earners take a little more out than the other groups – around £225,000 at 2001 prices (about £320,000 in 2013 prices) – but everyone else takes benefits and services worth around £200,000 (equivalent to about £280,000 at 2013 prices).[9]

Obviously, people in the richer groups tend to pay a lot more towards the cost of the welfare state in the course of their lifetimes than the poorer groups do, so most of them end up making a net loss on their tax/welfare accounts while most of those in the poorer groups make a net gain. This can be seen in Fig.1b ('Net lifetime taxes and average net gain') where the shaded bars indicate the average amount of tax paid in a lifetime, over and above the value of the welfare benefits and services consumed. We can see that the individuals who make up the richest decile are on average paying almost £200,000 in net tax. Put another way, they not only pay for their own benefits and services, but they contribute almost as much again towards the cost of other people's.

Fig.1b shows that on average, the people in the four richest lifetime deciles make a loss on their tax/welfare balances (they pay in more than they take out, shown by the dotted line remaining in negative territory), while those in the poorest five make a profit (they take out more than they pay in, signified by the dotted line rising into the positive segment of the graph). On average, the individuals in the sixth lifetime income decile break even. There is clearly redistribution going on, therefore, between higher and lower income groups over their lifetimes.

The most interesting feature of Fig.1, however, is the breakdown in each of the bars in the top graph (part a) between 'self-financed benefits' (the shaded segment) and 'net lifetime benefits' (the blocked segment). This reveals that in *every* income decile, people are on average paying taxes in the course of their lifetimes which cover a hefty chunk of the welfare benefits and services they consume. Even the individuals who over their lifetimes make up the poorest 10 per cent of the population on average self-finance almost *half* of all the benefits and services they receive; the next decile up self-finances two-thirds of them.[10]

Hills calculates that the average person in the course of a lifetime self-finances 74 per cent of everything they draw out of the welfare system. The situation is rather like that experienced by Tony Hancock in the famous *Blood Donor* sketch: having paid into the system earlier, we return later to claim most of our contributions back again.

Hills prefers a different metaphor: '*Most* benefits are self-financed over people's lifetimes, rather than being paid for by others. On these results, nearly three-quarters of what the welfare state was doing in the late 1980s and early 1990s was like a "savings bank", and only a quarter was "Robin Hood" redistribution between different people.'[11]

So while it is true (as Beveridge recognised) that there will always need to be some taxpayer-funded 'social assistance' for people who will never earn enough in a lifetime to pay for all the benefits and services they need (the 'Robin Hood' redistribution that Hills discusses), it is also clearly the case that most of us could afford to pay for most of our own lifetime maintenance if some way could be found to reduce the amount of tax the state takes from us to pay for the welfare it insists on giving us (the 'savings bank' function). With the appropriate income-smoothing instruments in place – savings accounts, loan facilities and insurance policies – most households could on these figures finance most of their lifetime welfare needs through their own contributions.

It seems from this that the contributory principle is not doomed after all, for many of us are still contributing handsomely towards the cost of our own benefits. It's just that it doesn't look that way because the government handles all the money flows on our behalf.

The true situation would be more obvious if, instead of paying into one, big government pot, we separated out the money we pay for redistribution to other people from the money we pay to finance our own future needs. The first set of payments would take the form of tax deductions which would be used to fund targeted welfare benefits for other people less fortunate than ourselves; for the average person, this would absorb just one-quarter of the taxes they currently pay. The second set of payments would go straight into our own, personal, welfare accounts, where it would be used to buy a retirement annuity, purchase health insurance, and build up savings to be used if and when our earnings are interrupted by some misfortune. For the average person, this personal welfare account would absorb the other three-quarters of the money they currently give the government in taxes.

Means-testing benefits to make room for more self-provisioning

The high level of lifetime tax/welfare churning in Britain (74 per cent of payments recycled on average) is not unusual by international standards. In every advanced welfare state, when we track taxes and benefits over people's entire lifetimes, we find a large proportion of the taxes they pay towards the cost of the welfare state is sooner or later returned to them in cash or in kind, rather than being redistributed to other people.

It is noticeable, however, that in countries which rely

more heavily on means-testing, tax/welfare churning tends to be lower. In Australia, for example, there is no social insurance system, and never has been. All benefits are paid out of general taxation, and many (including family benefits and the age pension) are means-tested to limit them to less affluent claimants. The result is that 'only' around half of welfare state spending is churned (although Australians in the bottom decile of lifetime earnings still end up paying in direct taxes for half of all the cash benefits they receive from their government).[12]

In continental Europe, by contrast, universal benefits are more common and entitlement is more often based on social insurance contributions. The consequence is that tax/welfare churning tends to be much more extensive. In Denmark, Italy and Sweden, between 74 per cent and 76 per cent of the money collected in taxes to finance social insurance payments is channelled back at some point to those who contributed it, and when state health and education spending is included (as it needs to be to achieve comparability with Hills's UK data), the proportion of the welfare budget that is churned rises even higher (in Sweden to an estimated 82 per cent).[13]

The contrast between Australia and, say, Sweden shows that, when state assistance is means-tested, government welfare spending tends to be lower, which makes the tax burden less onerous. Australian state and federal governments spend about 24 per cent of the nation's GDP on provisions like health care, education, housing and transfer payments (benefits and pensions). This is remarkably low by European standards (the comparable figure is 29 per cent in the UK, and above 35 per cent in France, Belgium, Denmark and Sweden), yet income redistribution by means of tax and welfare is actually more extensive in Australia than in most European countries.[14] Inter-personal redistribution is unaffected by Australia's lower level of state spending; it is the intra-personal redistribution that is reduced – mainly by means-testing the state age pension.

Because people retain more of their own income in Australia, they can make greater provision for themselves and their families than is the norm in Europe. Home ownership is more widespread, private medical insurance coverage is higher, the number of children attending non-state schools is greater (although school fees are often heavily subsidised by taxpayers), and (because of the compulsory superannuation scheme) savings in personal retirement accounts are larger and more extensive.

Making self-provisioning compulsory

On its own, means-testing is a blunt instrument for reducing tax/welfare churning, for as critics like Frank Field have been arguing for many years, it generates perverse incentives by rewarding people for being needy. It discourages saving and penalises work, even though this was never the intention.[15]

If Britain started means-testing the state retirement pension, everybody would know they would qualify for a pension provided they have no retirement savings of their own. Inevitably, the result would be that some people would not bother to save at all, preferring to rely on others to bail them out when the time comes to stop working. Means-testing could in this way prove counter-productive by discouraging saving and rewarding free riders.

The most effective way to counter this free-rider problem would be to force everyone who is able to do so to make provision for themselves. If you are forced to pay into your own pension fund (or other welfare account, for that matter), the option is no longer available to avoid saving in order to qualify for a means-tested state pension. Only those people who have for some legitimate reason been unable to build up savings during their working lives will then be eligible to claim state support. This is precisely the strategy adopted by Australia when it introduced its compulsory Superannuation Guarantee scheme in 1992.

To strengthen the contributory principle, therefore, we need *both* means-testing *and* compulsory saving. Means-testing is needed to target state benefits more precisely on those in need, leaving other people to use their own contributions to pay for their needs. Compulsory saving is needed to ensure that people who could make provision for themselves do so, and do not end up claiming state assistance instead.

This two-fold strategy of means-testing coupled with mandatory saving mirrors what Beveridge set out to achieve in his great reforms seventy years ago. He devised a compulsory system of saving (National Insurance contributions) to run alongside a means-tested safety net of National Assistance. National Insurance was to function as a system of lifetime income smoothing based on regular contributions from people in work, and it had no role to play in redistribution (which is why Beveridge insisted on flat-rate contributions and benefits). Meanwhile, means-tested national assistance was envisaged as a subsidiary back-up, financed out of taxation, and intended for those with no or inadequate entitlements. Most people of working age were expected to finance most, if not all, of their own welfare benefits, including their retirement pension, through their (or their partner's) own contributions.

We saw in Part II that this system has all but broken down now, but this is not because the principle itself was flawed. It is rather because Beveridge organised the payment and management of contributions through a government fund, rather than allowing people to accumulate and manage their own contributions in their own, personal funds.

There was nothing wrong with requiring workers

to make regular contributions to cover the cost of their own subsistence at times of sickness, unemployment and retirement. Even in the 1940s, most workers could afford to do this. Indeed, the history of the friendly societies shows that most could afford to do it back in the late nineteenth century.

We have seen from John Hills's analysis of lifetime income smoothing that most people could also afford to do it today, if they were not already paying huge sums in tax for the government to do it for them. Rising living standards over the last 70 years mean that many more people could in principle afford to provide for themselves now than in Beveridge's day.[16] And with more women in paid employment now, the problem of providing cover for uninsured dependents is also much less acute now than it was then.

Beveridge's mistake was not that he expected people to finance their own benefits, but that he made workers pay their contributions into a single insurance fund placed in the hands of the government. By pooling everybody's contributions in a government-run insurance scheme, rather than allowing individuals to build up their own savings accounts, he stripped people of the power and responsibility to organise their own lives, forced them instead to place their trust in politicians and bureaucrats who have continually fiddled with the rules and devalued future returns, and blunted the work and savings incentives which would have been created had individuals been given control of their own money.

With all the money pooled, National Insurance has turned into a classic example of the 'tragedy of the commons'.[17] Paying into a common fund maximises the temptation to get as much money out as possible for yourself while minimising the incentive to avoid running the fund down by excessive claiming. Everybody knows that the impact

RESCUING THE CONTRIBUTORY PRINCIPLE

on the fund's solvency of any one person's withdrawals is
infinitesimal ('the government can afford it'), and that if
they don't claim, other people still will ('you're a mug not
to'). All that holds claimants back from milking the system
is their personal honesty and integrity, coupled with strict
application of the rules by those with the responsibility for
assessing claims. In the end, neither of these safeguards has
proved strong enough.

Had people's contributions been kept in savings accounts
and managed in their own names, by contrast, there would
have been a much stronger incentive for people to husband
their accounts more responsibly, rather than exploiting the
shared pot.

Seventy years later, with the new system of workplace
pensions now being phased in by the government, we have
the opportunity to rectify Beveridge's error. But to do so,
saving in personal accounts needs to be made compulsory,
not left optional, as the new workplace pensions scheme
permits, and it needs to cover more than just retirement.

The case for individual accounts

There are five reasons why requiring people to manage
their own money in personal welfare accounts is preferable
to taxing them so the government can give them benefits
and services.[18]

The first is that it is more efficient. When the government
taxes people's earnings, and then returns their money to
them in the form of welfare benefits or services in kind,
it has to take a slice off the top to cover its administrative
costs. One bureaucracy is needed to take people's money
away, and another is needed to give it back again. We saw
in Part II that there are also 'compliance costs' for employers
who are required to act as unpaid tax collectors, and there

are 'enforcement costs' for government in detecting and chasing people who fraudulently claim benefits. Moving to a system of personal accounts should reduce all these costs and, other things being equal, should leave people better off than they are under the current system.

Of course, a shift from state-managed to privately-managed savings will itself incur some new administrative overheads, but competition between financial service providers should drive down costs and charges. Even if it doesn't, self-funding will reduce the expense entailed in detailed scrutiny of each individual's personal circumstances, for when people are drawing on their own funds, there is less need to check whether they are defrauding them. Welfare 'scrounging' under a system of personal accounts makes little sense, for those who claim unnecessarily are only defrauding themselves.

The second reason for favouring personal welfare accounts is that work disincentives are reduced by lowering taxation. People's net (take-home) incomes might be no different, for much of the money they save on taxes and NICs would have to be devoted to increased expenditure on things like unemployment insurance or savings for old age. It is therefore quite likely that people would be little or no better off than before once all their basic needs have been paid for.

But the incentive to work harder and save more would be strengthened because workers would be retaining control of their own money. Deductions from their wages would be going into their own personal funds rather than disappearing into the government treasury. They would be deferring income, but not losing it (and the money invested in personal accounts would grow over time).[19]

The third reason for favouring personal welfare accounts is that government social insurance schemes are becoming increasingly unsustainable. We saw in Part II that increased average life expectancy and lower fertility rates are leading to a shortfall in funding both for the state retirement pension (as the size of the working population shrinks relative to that of retirees) and government health care (as the elderly population puts added burdens on health and care services). By the turn of this century, the cost of the state pension and associated retirement benefits, if left unreformed, will rise from £84bn to £250bn (2012 prices).[20]

The government has responded to this by raising the retirement age and linking it to future increases in average life expectancy.[21] This will help stabilize the size of the retiree population, but it will do nothing to make their pension claims more affordable for a dwindling proportion of working taxpayers. A switch to self-funding (coupled with means-testing of those claiming a state pension) offers the best prospect of a long-term solution to this unaffordable and inexorable rise in government spending.[22]

It is important to be clear that, like state pensions, private retirement savings funds will still be vulnerable to a shrinking working-age population, for when individuals retire and seek to convert their bonds, shares or other assets into an income stream, there will be fewer workers around to buy these assets, leading to a fall in their value and lower retirement annuities.[23] However, unlike a Pay-As-You-Go state pension scheme, which can only draw on the output generated by British taxpayers, a private pension fund can invest across the globe, seeking out higher returns from countries with younger or more productive workforces. Retirement incomes are therefore likely to be higher if we make the switch from a state to personal funds.

The fourth argument for replacing state benefits with personal accounts is more psychological. By taking people's earnings away in tax, and then compensating them with welfare benefits and services in kind, politicians meet people's basic needs but neglect what psychologist Abraham

Maslow identified as their 'higher needs' for self-respect and 'self-actualisation'. Unlike food and shelter, these higher needs cannot be organised for us by politicians.

A sense of self-worth comes from accepting responsibility for yourself, and it is impossible to take pride in yourself if the government provides you with everything you need.[24] Similarly, self-actualisation (fulfillment of potential) requires that we achieve things through our own efforts, but the welfare state exists precisely to take personal challenges away. As a leading American welfare analyst puts it: 'The purpose of most social policies is to reduce a difficulty, lower a barrier, or insure against a risk.'[25]

The unintended result is too often what psychologists call 'learned helplessness.' Habituated to welfare, we come to expect the government to do something whenever a problem arises, rather than working out how to tackle it ourselves. This not only politicizes huge areas of life as we all squabble about who should get what; it also undermines one of the core conditions of human happiness and life satisfaction.[26] Beveridge understood this, which is why he placed the contributory principle at the core of his welfare design, and personal accounts exemplify this principle by allowing people to build up their own assets, rather than obliging them to go cap-in-hand to the government.[27]

The fifth and final reason for preferring a system of personal welfare accounts over conventional state welfare benefits is that they can promote the civic virtues which conventional state benefits tend to erode.

Chancellor George Osborne recently attracted criticism by suggesting that the welfare system was enabling destructive social behavior to flourish.[28] But he was right; despite the good intentions of social reformers down the years, the welfare state has encouraged social irresponsibility.[29] It has enabled men to disown responsibility for their children, fostered delinquency among disenchanted youths, and subsidised crime and incivility. As Labour MP Frank Field suggests, giving people money and services with little or nothing being demanded or expected in return has 'severed the connection between a person's actions and accepting the consequences of that pattern of behaviour.'[30]

People have stopped saving for their old age because they know the state will provide them with an income when they get older. They do not bother to insure against ill health because the government will provide free hospital care if calamity strikes. They engage in self-destructive behaviour, like substance abuse, knowing that the government will give them an income even if they make themselves unemployable. Men who father children they do not want know the government will support their families if they abandon them. In these, and many other similar ways, the welfare state reproduces the very problems it was intended to resolve.

By reinstating personal responsibility to the heart of social policy, personal accounts can begin to reverse this something-for-nothing welfare culture. They cannot magically restore our old civic culture of social responsibility, but they will at least help stop the rot.

Income smoothing without the state

There are three ways individuals can smooth out their incomes during the course of their lives without relying on the government. They can borrow, they can insure and they can save. This suggests that some combination of savings, insurance and loans would have to be developed if various aspects of the welfare state's current income smoothing function were to be devolved to individual households.

Savings are an appropriate replacement for state provision where future needs can be anticipated and planned for. The obvious example is the use of personal accounts to provide retirement income, although savings accounts need not be limited to providing pensions. They could also be used to meet the costs of everyday medical expenses, to pay for education or training courses taken later in life, to provide an income during brief periods out of the labour force due to sickness, unemployment or maternity, to provide a deposit to buy a house, or to pay school fees for one's children.

Saving is probably the most flexible and secure way of smoothing income over a long period, but it will not always prove the most appropriate. Where risks are small but potentially very costly if they do happen, it would be inefficient for everyone to save large sums on the off-chance that some disaster might befall them. In situations like this, insurance (pooled risk) is usually a better option. The risk of loss of earnings due to long-term sickness or disability, for example, is probably better covered by insurance than by personal saving. So too is the risk of needing expensive nursing home care in old age.

There are some well-known problems in insurance markets that would have to be overcome if these sorts of risks were to be covered by private insurers. One is 'adverse selection' (where only people who are seriously at risk bother to insure themselves). This drives up the cost of premiums as there are few policy-holders who do not end up making claims. Another is 'moral hazard', where insured people maximise their eligibility for benefits by putting themselves at risk – e.g. by making themselves unemployed, or failing to look seriously for another job, in order to qualify for unemployment insurance payments.

There are ways of overcoming both of these problems. Requiring everyone to insure themselves is a simple way of overcoming adverse selection, for it ensures that high and low risks alike are included in the pool. Once again, this points to the case for some element of government compulsion. Moral hazard can be minimised by offering no-claim bonus incentives, or by requiring claimants to pay a 'deductible' (the first £x) on any claim they do make. This discourages non-essential claims and reduces the cost of premiums.[31]

Loans are the mirror-image of savings, for they offer an appropriate way of funding costs incurred earlier in life, before individuals have accumulated much capital, but when they can still anticipate many years of future earnings. Students in higher education already take out loans to cover their university fees, for example, just as households already borrow substantial sums relatively early in life in order to buy housing, paying off the loan from later earnings.

In principle it might be possible to extend the use of loans into other areas of provision currently covered by welfare benefits, such as short-term unemployment. As we saw in Part I, loans to cover periods of unemployment were tried in the 1920s in Britain, when 'uncovenanted benefits' were introduced for unemployed workers who had exhausted their 15-week entitlement to welfare assistance. In practice, however, these advances were rarely repaid. But if every worker were making regular contributions to a compulsory personal welfare account, loans to cover short periods of unemployment or sickness could be secured against future payments into this account (although it would still be necessary to limit total indebtedness if spells of unemployment lengthen).

Using personal accounts for multiple purposes

There is nothing new about the idea that people should take more responsibility for smoothing their lifetime income flows by saving, insuring themselves, or borrowing against future earnings. Various commentators and think-tanks in Britain have proposed making greater use of personal welfare accounts to reduce our reliance on the state managing our incomes for us:

◆ Almost twenty years ago, the Adam Smith Institute proposed what it called compulsory 'Fortune Accounts' for every individual, to substitute for National Insurance. Personal savings, backed up where appropriate by government contributions, would accumulate in these accounts and be used both to fund retirement and to purchase insurance against risks like unemployment and sickness.[32]

◆ More recently, the Taxpayers' Alliance has proposed that compulsory superannuation accounts on the Australian model should be introduced with the long-term aim of replacing the state pension. It also argues that National Insurance should be scrapped and entitlement to contributory state benefits should be based on people's income tax payment records instead. [33]

◆ The free-market think tank Reform also favours a merger of National Insurance into income tax, with state pensions eventually being means-tested and paid out of tax revenues. Reform suggests the new workplace pensions could be extended into 'Personal Protection Accounts' with working-age people using them to cover risks like unemployment, disability and parenthood, as well as retirement, although it does not develop the idea in any detail.[34] As we saw above, Reform also believes that retirees should be required to draw on capital tied up in their housing as an alternative to relying on government benefits.[35]

◆ In 2013, Policy Exchange (said to be David Cameron's favourite think-tank) came out in favour of 'strengthening the contributory principle through a system of welfare accounts that sit on top of the universal credit and that can be drawn down in periods of need', although this suggestion has yet to be fleshed out in a fully-worked proposal.[36]

Many of these proposals envisage some combination of personal retirement savings with unemployment, disability and possibly health risk cover organised by means of insurance and loans. Nobel Prize-winning economist, Joseph Stiglitz, has demonstrated that integrating these different risks through one savings account is generally a better strategy than keeping them separate, for it maximises income security while minimising moral hazard problems.[37] The obvious danger with integration is that people might draw so heavily on their savings during their working lives that they are left with insufficient funds in their accounts when they retire. However, Stiglitz shows that integration in a single account creates a strong incentive not to draw on the money unless it is absolutely necessary to do so (because people do not want to squander their retirement nest eggs).[38] He therefore proposes what he calls an 'integrated lifetime insurance programme' which rolls the risks of retirement, unemployment, disability and health into a single personal account with multiple purposes.[39] He cites the Provident Funds of Singapore and Malaysia (discussed below) as examples of what he has in mind.

It is important to emphasise that increased use of savings, insurance and loans to reduce lifetime churning does not rule out a continuing role for government. Governments might top up people's purchasing power (e.g. by making a co-contribution to their personal pension plans, or by offering tax relief on contributions), they might underwrite high-risk insurance, and they might offer tax reimbursements for those who opt for a private sector alternative rather than using an existing government service. Government also has a crucial regulatory role in ensuring that people do make provision for themselves, and it will always need to provide back-up assistance for those who cannot support themselves, e.g. through means-tested state pensions for those with fractured employment histories, or unconditional benefits for severely disabled people who cannot work.

Making a start: Automatic enrolment in workplace pensions

In 2010-11, just 35 per cent of working-age people in Britain were contributing to a private pension scheme of some kind. Six million were paying into a personal scheme such as a Stakeholder Pension or a Self-Invested Pension (down from 6.4 million two years earlier), and 8.3 million (5.3 million of them being public sector employees) were in occupational schemes organised by their employers (the lowest proportion since records began in 1953).[40] Both trend lines show that, rather than progressing towards greater self-reliance in retirement, we have been going backwards.

A number of factors have contributed to this fall in private pension membership. Employers outside the public sector have been closing their defined-benefit schemes which have become cripplingly expensive; the last Labour government siphoned £5bn per year out of people's pension pots by taxing dividends paid on shares held in pension funds; and the collapse in interest rates created by the credit crunch (and exacerbated by the Coalition government's 'quantitative easing' measures) has made annuities purchased with retirement savings look extremely unattractive. The government estimated in 2012 that some 11 million workers were failing to save enough to provide themselves with an adequate income in retirement.[41]

The government's response to this fall in personal retirement saving came in the 2008 Pensions Act which requires all employers in Britain to offer their employees a defined-contribution 'workplace pension' which must meet certain minimum standards. Employers may set up their own scheme, or they can default to the National Employment Savings Trust (NEST) scheme which is guaranteed to meet the mandated conditions. (NEST has been established by statute as an independent trust answerable to the Department of Work and Pensions.)[42]

Workplace pensions are being phased in with different deadlines for large and small companies, but, by 2018, every employer in the country must be offering one. By that time, the minimum employee contribution (which is eligible for tax relief) will be eight per cent of salary, with an annual contributions limit of £4,500 (indexed at 2013/14 prices). Employers will be required to contribute an additional three per cent of everything their employees earn up to £35,782 pa, bringing the total pension contribution for most workers to 11 per cent of salary (6.4 per cent from the employee, 1.6 per cent from the taxpayer, and 3 per cent from the employer).

Savings can be accessed on retirement provided employees have reached the age of 55. Up to a quarter of the total may be taken as a tax-free lump-sum with the rest used to buy an annuity. (If retirees have other private pension income, more of the workplace pension may be redeemable as cash.)

Not every employee will be joining a workplace pension scheme. Participation by part-time and young workers on low incomes is entirely a matter for them.[43] And although all other workers (so-called 'eligible jobholders') must be automatically enrolled by their employers, they can opt out if they wish. The Act requires employers to enrol every member of their workforce who is (a) over 22 and below retirement age, (b) not already in a comparable scheme, and (c) earning above £8,105 p.a. But employees are free to leave the scheme at any time. The government hopes to 'nudge' people into retirement saving, not compel them.[44]

It is tempting to dismiss this new system as too little, too late.

It has arguably come too late because the post-war birth bulge – the 'baby boomers' – are already retiring. The crisis of an ageing population is upon us. Yet even as the ratio of retired to employed workers is rising, we have seen that personal retirement savings have been plummeting. A move like this should have been made decades ago, when the economic climate would also have been more auspicious.

It is arguably too little because 11 per cent of earnings may not be enough to give people an adequate retirement income without relying on state top-ups.[45] Total contributions to traditional final salary pension schemes average 21 per cent of earnings.[46] It seems the state pension will remain the primary source of retirement income for many people, with the workplace pension as a top-up, when the reverse pattern is what is really needed. What is more, the right to opt out of the workplace pension means some people (arguably those with the least foresight and the least-developed sense of personal responsibility) won't save at all.

Again, Australia can furnish useful evidence. There, nine per cent of people's salary packages is deducted for personal superannuation, and this is compulsory for all workers. But this figure is widely acknowledged to be too small, and the rate is now being raised to 12 per cent. But as we saw earlier, even when Australia's superannuation scheme has fully matured in the middle of this century, three-quarters of retirees will still qualify for a (part or full) means-tested state pension to top them up.[47]

Of course, workers enrolled in workplace pensions can

choose to contribute more than the minimum, or to augment their retirement savings in other ways. For those who spend most of their lives in work, and who choose to remain in the scheme, the combination of the state pension and a workplace pension should ensure a reasonably comfortable retirement. But workplace pensions are piggy-backing on the universal, basic state pension, not substituting for it.

Nevertheless, they are an important start, and they provide a basis on which we can begin to rebuild the contributory principle, not only to cover retirement pensions, but in working-life benefits too.

Unlike National Insurance, where the money workers pay in is paid straight out again to other people, workplace pension contributions will build up in members' own accounts. The pension will be portable, so it will follow workers when they change jobs. People can go on-line and see how their fund is progressing (including any profits it may be accruing). They can receive annual statements projecting the likely value of their pension when they retire. It is their money, and nobody else (including the government) can touch it. This is a vital first step in establishing personal responsibility for lifetime income smoothing.

Making workplace pensions compulsory

The essential next step is to make participation in workplace pensions compulsory for all employees.

Libertarians generally oppose making retirement saving compulsory. They dislike the strong element of state paternalism this entails, and they worry that workers may be forced to save inefficiently when they might do a lot better investing their money in other ways.[48] In this view, it is better to allow people the freedom to determine how best to spend or save their own money, even if this results in some making bad choices, and others making no provision at all for their old age.

Such arguments are often countered by asking what happens when people who have been allowed to make their own mistakes end up needing other people's help. When the rest of us see elderly people in financial difficulties, we will come under irresistible moral and political pressure to do something to alleviate their suffering, even if their predicament is entirely their own fault. That being the case, it makes sense to ensure that everyone who is working puts enough money aside for themselves and their dependents so they won't have to seek help from the state.[49]

In the UK, however, the government already guarantees almost everybody a minimum retirement income, irrespective of whether they have savings of their own. As we saw in Part II, British retirees will in future receive around £145 p.w., regardless of their National Insurance contributions record, for those who have being paying in will get their full pension entitlement (which in future will include the former second state pension), while those who have made no contributions and have no other source of private income will be able to claim Pension Credit worth almost the same amount. In this context, the new workplace pensions represent an additional source of income in retirement, so even if some people opt out of them, they should not end up in such dire financial straits that future taxpayers will need to give them any more than they are already entitled to.

There is, however, still a compelling argument for requiring people to save for their own retirement, and this is that the unfunded liabilities of the state pension scheme are now so large that it is difficult to see how future state pensions can realistically be paid unless people start to take more responsibility for their own retirement.

The UK government currently owes over £5.0 trillion

in pension obligations. Nearly all of this (£4.7 trillion) is unfunded. This debt is the equivalent of 342 per cent of the nation's current GDP.[50]

£3.8 trillion of this pension debt (263 per cent of the country's GDP) is made up of future state pension payments. This is after allowing for recent changes to the minimum retirement age intended to ease the burden of financing future state pension payments. All of this money will have to be paid by future taxpayers, for there is no accumulated National Insurance fund to draw on. In addition, the government owes £0.9 trillion (58 per cent of GDP) in unfunded pension obligations to its own public sector employees, and £1.2 trillion (80 per cent of GDP) in its contributions to workplace pension schemes which are also largely unfunded.

None of this debt is included in official estimates of the size of the national debt (currently running at just over £1 trillion, or £38,000 for every UK household).[51] When these future pension obligations are added, as they probably should be, the size of government debt balloons, averaging out at £130,000 of debt for every UK household.[52] The great bulk of this is represented by the state pension.

Seen in this light, means-testing the state pension (a policy advocated in Part II) is not only a sensible and desirable policy; it may be an unavoidable one. A recent survey found that nearly half of the country's leading economists believe that the state pension will have to be means-tested by the year 2040.[53]

Means-testing the state pension is only viable if personal retirement saving is made mandatory. As we saw earlier, if people are able to opt out of saving in their own workplace pensions, means-testing the state basic pension would create strong moral hazard problems (for those who opt out know they will be rescued by taxpayers). Getting people to take more responsibility for themselves, and weaning the nation off its dependency on government benefits, thus requires both a means-tested state pension and a mandatory private one.

Britain would not be alone in compelling people to save for their retirement in their own personal accounts. We have already seen that Australia introduced compulsory superannuation for all employees as long ago as 1992. Today, more than four in every five Australian workers are in a scheme (membership is not compulsory for the self-employed), and there are over 200,000 different funds (although two-thirds of assets are concentrated in the one hundred biggest funds).[54]

Compulsory retirement saving accounts of various kinds have been introduced in many other countries too over the last twenty or thirty years. A 2005 review identified 31 countries which had implemented some form of compulsory personal account as part of their pension system.[55] Most combine it with some form of state pension, although a few (mainly in Central and South America) have it as their only statutory retirement savings scheme. Of those that combine state pensions with private savings, most have the former as the principal instrument with the latter as a supplement. They include several EU countries such as Italy and Poland. Since 1998, Sweden has allowed workers to use 2.5 per cent of their 18.5 per cent social insurance payments to fund so-called 'premium accounts' which they manage themselves, while the bulk of their contributions still fund the PAYG state pension. [56]

Additional uses for personal savings accounts: lessons from Chile and Singapore

The first, and probably best-known, compulsory, personal, retirement savings scheme was established in Singapore in

1955, when it was still under British colonial rule. Strictly speaking, it is not a system of personal accounts as such, for individuals cannot choose where to put their money, and they have no say in managing their funds. Rather, workers and their employers are required to deposit a percentage of monthly earnings (up to a specified income limit) into individually-earmarked accounts run by a government-managed Central Provident Fund (CPF). The CPF then invests this money on their behalf.[57] But although the state controls the money while it is on deposit, ownership is still vested in individual contributors, and it can be bequeathed or shared among family members.

The original scheme has expanded considerably in scope as well as size since the 1950s. Today, it has 3.4 million members, covering about two-thirds of the labour force (foreign, part-time, causal and self-employed workers are exempt but may make voluntary contributions).[58]

In 1965 the scheme was expanded to allow members to use part of their funds (placed in an 'ordinary account') to pay for the purchase of a state-built apartment. In 1984, another section of each savings account was created (known as 'Medisave') to be used for payment of hospital and certain other medical expenses.[59] And in 1986, the function of the ordinary accounts was expanded to allow members to use them to invest in stocks approved by the Provident Fund. Ordinary accounts may also be used to buy home protection insurance and dependents' protection insurance (in the event of death or incapacity of the principal earner), and to pay college education expenses.[60]

At its inception, employees and employers each paid 10 per cent of the employee's net wages into the fund, but as the fund's purposes have expanded, so contribution levels have grown.[61] Since 2012, most participants have had to pay 36 per cent of their total wage into their accounts (20 per cent from the employee and 16 per cent from the employer), but contributions are lower for those over the age of 50.

These contributions are split between the three linked funds: 'special' accounts, which take between 6 per cent and 9.5 per cent of salary, are used to finance retirement; personal medical savings (Medisave) accounts, used to pay for hospital expenses and other approved medical insurance, take between 7 per cent and 9.5 per cent; and 'Ordinary Accounts' (absorbing 12 per cent to 23 per cent of salary, depending on the member's age) can be used for a variety of purposes including house purchase, education, insurance and investment.[62] Once people have saved enough in their special (retirement) and Medisave accounts to cover their retirement and health needs, further deposits can be used to boost personal investments through their ordinary accounts. All deposits, withdrawals and interest earned are free of tax, and all savings earn a minimum interest rate of 2.5 per cent which is guaranteed by the government, but the government makes no further contribution.[63]

In 1981, Chile followed Singapore's example by introducing a privatised retirement pensions system, but unlike Singapore, this involved a transition from an existing pay-as-you-go state system, which was threatening to collapse into insolvency. In 1924, Chile was the first western country to introduce a pay-as-you-go contributory state pension scheme; in 1981, it became the first to abandon one.[64] Workers were offered the option of remaining in the old state system if they preferred, but despite trade union opposition, more than nine out of ten of those eligible to move did so, and most of the rest followed soon after.[65] Their existing state pension entitlements were turned into government 'recognition bonds' which could be cashed on retirement.

As in Singapore, workers participating in the new scheme were required to pay a proportion of their earnings (minimum ten per cent, with up to another ten per cent optional) into a private account, but unlike Singapore, they could choose between competing fund management organisations and could switch between them to maximise their returns. As in Singapore, the Chilean government does not contribute to these funds, but it does guarantee the pensions they pay and promises to make up any shortfall when people reach retirement age. Thirty years on, that guarantee has never had to be activated.[66]

Just like in Singapore, once the Chilean scheme got firmly established, its functions began to expand. In 2002, a new Unemployment Insurance scheme was introduced which requires workers (0.6 per cent of monthly salary) and their employers (1.6 per cent) to make contributions to individual employee Unemployment Savings Accounts. In addition, a common Solidarity Fund is financed by employers (another 0.8 per cent) and government. When they become unemployed, workers must first draw down on their own unemployment savings accounts, and only when they are depleted can they turn to the solidarity fund.[67]

Neither of these flagship compulsory personal savings schemes has been without its problems. In Singapore, withdrawals to pay for home ownership have depleted some people's accounts to a level which may be insufficient to purchase an adequate retirement annuity.[68] Nor do workers have any say over how or where their money is invested. In Chile, where workers do have a choice between competing private sector fund managers, high fees can deplete deposits and effective coverage is patchy because most casual and temporary workers do not belong to any scheme.[69]

But on balance, both schemes have been very successful. The architect of the Chilean reform, Jose Pinera, claims that retirement pensions are 40 or 50 per cent higher than under the old system, and the average rate of return achieved by funds has been in excess of ten per cent per annum.[70] The average saver retires on 78 per cent of their previous income. Furthermore, a huge pool of savings has been generated which has provided the investment capital needed to sustain rapid economic growth, and which is predicted to total 134 per cent of GDP by 2020.[71] The stark contrast with Britain's crushing pensions deficit is striking.

Using savings accounts for short periods of unemployment, sickness and parental leave

It is obviously important not to overload personal savings accounts.[72] In both Chile and Singapore, they started life purely as retirement savings vehicles and only later were extended to cover other needs, such as unemployment, medical and house purchase, once people had begun to accumulate substantial reserves in their funds. Nevertheless, the Chile and Singapore cases do suggest that, once workplace pensions are up and running in the UK in 2018 (and assuming that saving in these accounts is made compulsory), more functions could start to be added.

Risks which are currently covered by state benefits but which might lend themselves best to a savings model are those where there is currently a high level of lifetime income churning (i.e. where most people end up financing most of the state benefits they claim through their own tax payments). Danish research suggests that child benefits, parental leave benefits, higher education grants and short-term sickness and unemployment benefits all fall into this category, which makes them all potential candidates for transfer to personal accounts.[73]

Personal accounts are also particularly suitable for covering non-catastrophic risks, like short-term unemployment and sickness, where external verification of people's circumstances is difficult and costly.[74] Requiring people to fund absences from work from their own savings, rather than drawing on taxpayer-funded benefits, creates an incentive not to claim unless the condition is genuine (since fraudsters will only be using up their own funds). It may not even be necessary to check up on people claiming to be unemployed or sick for short periods for as long as they are living from their own savings accounts.

Given the primary purpose of personal accounts is to fund retirement, however, it is important to have rules limiting the size and duration of withdrawals made during people's working lives, to prevent them using up all their savings by the time they retire. The maximum income drawn from personal welfare accounts during any period away from work should be no greater than the state benefit to which an equivalent person would be entitled under existing arrangements. The duration for which someone is entitled to withdraw money should also be limited so accounts do not get drained too rapidly. But within these constraints, personal accounts could go a long way to reducing reliance on state-provided working-age benefits and strengthening self-reliance.

One obvious risk that might be covered is temporary unemployment. Most periods of unemployment are of relatively short duration: in the UK in 2013, just over half of Jobseeker's Allowance claims lasted for less than six months.[75] The impact on their pension savings if people were allowed to use these accounts to cover average-length periods of unemployment should not therefore be too damaging. Stiglitz calculates that three spells of unemployment over 45 years of a working life, each spell lasting less than six months, will deplete someone's lifetime income by only about four per cent. He concludes that a personal savings account should 'easily' be able to absorb such a loss and still fund a decent pension in retirement.

Absence from work due to sickness might also be covered by drawing an income from personal savings accounts. Sickness-related absences are generally much shorter than spells of unemployment, averaging about six days per illness for workers in the private sector, and nine for those in the public sector. On average, just 1.5 per cent of scheduled working days are lost to sickness, so again, this should not make too big a dent in personal account balances.[76]

We might even allow workers to fund short periods of parental leave from their personal accounts.[77] At the moment, parents with young children have a right to take up to four weeks per year off work to look after their children (e.g. when day care arrangements break down, or children are ill), but such absences are unpaid (unless employers choose to cover them). With a system of personal accounts in place, parents would have the option of drawing on some of their savings to make up for some of this loss of income.

In all these cases, the great advantage of switching from reliance on welfare benefits to use of a personal savings account is that it substantially reduces work disincentives. When you are using up your own savings during absences from work, rather than claiming government money, you are more likely to want to return to work as soon as you can. This has the potential significantly to reduce demand on remaining state welfare budgets.[78]

There is strong evidence, both from economic modelling and from the experience of countries that have introduced personal unemployment savings accounts, that reliance on personal savings reduces the time people spend out of work. In Chile, the more money unemployed people have in their personal Unemployment Savings Accounts (hence the more they stand to lose during periods of joblessness), the quicker they find another job. Those who rely on the state Solidarity Fund for support remain unemployed for longer than those who draw on their own Unemployment

Savings Accounts.[79]

The obvious disadvantage, however, is that some people may not have sufficient money in their savings accounts to give them the temporary income they need. They may be young workers who have not had time to build up their funds, or people who have recently depleted their funds to cover loss of earnings during other recent periods of joblessness. In cases like these, some back-up provision is obviously required.

Loans to supplement savings

One possible back-up is to allow people with insufficient savings to borrow to cover their living expenses during short jobless periods, with loans being secured on their future earnings. Effectively, this already happens in the case of higher education students who borrow to pay tuition fees on the strength of their likely future earnings. They repay their loans when they get into employment and start to earn a reasonable income. There is no reason why a similar principle should not also apply to people who spend time out of the labour market for reasons other than studying.

Those whose personal welfare savings funds were depleted might be allowed to go into deficit for the duration of their period of joblessness, be it caused by sickness, unemployment or leave. The debt would then be cleared when they returned to work and resumed making regular, compulsory contributions. In this way, even those with no money in their savings accounts could still take responsibility for themselves rather than relying on handouts from taxpayers.[80]

The 2005 film *Cinderella Man* tells the true story of American boxer Jim Braddock, who was world heavyweight champion in 1935-37. Braddock lost all his savings in the

1929 Wall Street crash, then lost his livelihood when his boxing licence was revoked after a broken hand led to a string of defeats. After selling everything of value he owned, including his boxing kit, he eventually swallowed his pride, stood in line at the welfare office, and solicited an emergency welfare payment so he could get his electricity and gas reconnected. Later, after he won a comeback bout, he returned to the relief office, queued up again, and handed back the money he had been given.

Braddock's repayment of his benefit is a vivid expression of an ethic of personal responsibility which could be resuscitated by the development of personal accounts. In Sweden, unemployment benefits are already expected to be repaid by claimants who find work within six months.[81]

But what if people keep borrowing and never pay back? In the USA, it is estimated that if everyone had their own combined retirement and unemployment savings account, no more than five per cent to seven per cent would be in debt when they reach retirement age. In Sweden, researchers have found that even if people had to fund all their own working-age benefits – including sickness, maternity leave, child support, rent allowances and disability as well as unemployment – out of their own savings, only about 15 per cent to 17 per cent of accounts would be in the red at retirement.[82] Nevertheless, both of these simulations indicate that for a small minority of workers, self-funding could eat up all lifetime savings and put them in debt at the end of their working lives. So what then should happen?

Some people say debts should be forgiven when people retire.[83] This is essentially what happens in Chile. But this creates huge, potential moral hazard problems (allow your debt to build up, knowing that it will eventually be written off). It also creates unfairness with respect to other workers who do pay off their debts, only to find they also have to pay extra tax to cover other people's defaults and pensions.

It is clearly better not to allow large debts to accumulate in the first place. This means loans should only be made available up to a certain limit (either a financial cap, or a time limit). Once jobless people reach this limit, they should start claiming taxpayer-funded benefits (nowadays, the new universal credit).

The residual role of taxpayer-funded benefits for working-age claimants

Simulations suggest that, if we all had to save in personal accounts to cover some or all of the risks which are currently covered by the welfare state, the tax savings would be substantial. If all workers in the USA had their own combined unemployment and pensions saving accounts, the cost to the government of paying unemployment benefits would fall by 60 per cent. In Sweden, if workers had to cover all their working-age benefits out of savings, taxes could be cut by 30 per cent.[84]

Clearly, however, some working-age people will always need access to tax-funded benefits. People with severe disabilities are an obvious example. Under current rules, individuals with a 'substantially reduced capacity for working' are eligible to claim Employment and Support Allowance (formerly Incapacity Benefit), and if allocated to the 'Support Group' are not required to undertake any work-related activity.[85] A move to personal welfare savings accounts would not alter this, for people with permanent or long-term disabilities which prevent them from working are unlikely to be able to undertake the sustained periods of employment needed to build up savings or pay off loans.[86]

For people of working age who are capable of working, however, some combination of savings, loans and insurance should ideally become the primary method for providing an income when employment is temporarily disrupted. Only if personal welfare funds are exhausted should people resort to claiming taxpayer-funded benefits, and when they do, conditions should be attached to the receipt of these payments which clearly demarcate them from money drawn on a personal welfare account.

We saw in Part I how fairness requires that jobless people who contribute to the cost of their own maintenance should always be in a better position than those who do not. One way of achieving this might be to pay higher benefits to those who have been working and paying taxes in the past (something the Labour Party is currently considering).[87] But this would be expensive,[88] and it would, of course, no longer be an option if we moved to a system of personal accounts where people are using their own money to support themselves.

A better way of privileging those who fund themselves is to exempt them from activity conditions applied to those receiving government payments. We saw in Part I that this was Beveridge's favoured strategy, although the sharp distinction between contributory and non-contributory claims that he advocated has collapsed in later years. Restoring it would require that claimants in receipt of state benefits should normally undertake some kind of workfare activity, while those who maintain themselves using their own welfare savings accounts should not.

The main reason for imposing activity conditions on those claiming government benefits is that they strongly incentivise the return to work. Critics of workfare often complain that participants gain little or nothing from undertaking these activities, but the main impact of workfare programmes comes not from participating in them (the so-called 'programme effect'), but from claimants' desire to avoid them (the 'compliance' or 'deterrence' effect).[89]

Faced with a demand that they participate in an

intensive 'work-related activity' in return for their benefit, people step up their efforts to get a job. Whenever activity conditions are applied to welfare claims, the average duration of unemployment shortens and employment entry rates rise.[90] Merely insisting that applicants attend an initial interview typically leads to a reduction in welfare claims of five to ten per cent.[91] When the activity condition entails actual work, the flight from welfare is even more pronounced. In two under-reported UK pilots carried out in 1997, unemployment claims fell 25 per cent when a workfare trial was introduced.[92] When 'Work for the Dole' was introduced in Australia, one-third of those who were referred to it chose to give up their claim rather than work for their benefit.[93]

This strong compliance effect is the main reason for insisting that people claiming state benefits should be given activity tasks to perform. But it should not apply to those drawing on their own welfare savings accounts, for they already have a strong incentive to look for work: they do not want to deplete their funds.

There is therefore a strong moral and practical case for requiring those who seek state aid to participate from an early point in their claim in intensive work-related activity in return for their benefits. Those using their own welfare savings accounts, by contrast, should be allowed, say, six months to look for new, suitable employment for themselves, and during this period there should be no other activity requirement placed upon them. This would bring the benefits system back closer to what Beveridge had in mind in the 1940s when he outlined his plans for a rights-based contributory insurance system backed up by conditional public assistance.

Using savings accounts to contribute to routine health care costs

If people can save enough to pay for their own retirement needs, could they also save to meet the cost of lifetime health care or old-age nursing home fees? In both cases, the state budget is coming under increasing pressure, so the possibility that individuals might be able to assume more responsibility for funding themselves is obviously worth exploring.

The biggest problem with requiring people to save for items like health or old age care is that none of us knows how much money we will require in the future. Some people (those who avoid serious illness and do not require nursing home care when they get old) will end up saving much more than they need. Other, unluckier people will end up requiring more costly treatment and support than they could possibly be expected to save, even in a lifetime of earning.

The problem of 'over-saving' could be rectified by allowing savers to transfer surplus funds to other purposes. Singapore, for example, allows surplus health savings to be used for other purposes once people pass the age of 55. The second problem is, however, more worrying. What happens if somebody requires expensive medical treatment, or needs extended nursing home care, and has exhausted all their savings?

Clearly, funding of expensive but uncertain risks like these is better covered by insurance than by saving. In Britain, the National Health Service (NHS) functions as a compulsory common insurer, offering mainly 'free' health care treatment (funded out of general taxation) to everyone who needs it (albeit with rationing imposed through waiting lists and access regulated by gatekeepers like GPs). But like the state pension, the NHS budget has come under increasing pressure as the population ages and as new, expensive treatments and drugs become available, and this raises the question of whether personal accounts might help to relieve some of this pressure.

One way forward could be to require people in future to cover a proportion of their health-care expenses from their welfare savings accounts (or if they prefer, from their own pockets), leaving the NHS to pay the balance where health care bills go beyond a certain maximum threshold (say, £500 or £1,000 p.a.). This would be akin to payment of a 'deductible' in a commercial insurance policy, and it would have much the same effect. If the individual absorbs part of the cost, he or she is less likely to make trivial claims on the system, and the cost of financing the treatment they do need will fall because they are contributing something towards it.

Alternatively, we might be expected to use our personal accounts to pay some of our everyday medical bills, such as prescriptions or visits to the GP, and/or to cover the ancillary expenses of our treatment (such as 'hotel charges' incurred during hospital stays), while still relying on the 'insurance' offered by the NHS to cover us for more expensive items, such as hospital operations or treatment of long-term, chronic conditions. [94]

Requiring people to contribute something towards the cost of their medical expenses by drawing on their welfare savings accounts could drive down NHS costs and help put the service on a stronger long-term footing. People might start demanding that their GPs prescribe cheaper medicines: in South Africa, where personal Medical Savings Accounts have existed since 1992, people who pay for their medicines using their own accounts end up paying 11 per cent less on average for their prescription drugs.[95] They might take better care of themselves: in Singapore, where 'Medisave' has been running since 1984, health costs have stayed remarkably low by international standards, yet health outcomes measured by indicators like the infant mortality rate are extremely positive.[96] And the element of payment would almost certainly reduce unnecessary or trivial use of NHS resources which are currently free at the point of use, and therefore often abused.[97]

Whether a move like this is politically feasible is, however, another question. It would take a brave political party to propose that patients should use some of their own money to pay for some of the treatment they receive. Moreover, people without personal accounts (e.g. those who are severely disabled or retired from work) would be exempt from these payments, and they would probably be among the principal users of the NHS, so potential savings may not be large. At some point in the future, personal accounts could evolve to include an element of medical savings, but for the foreseeable future, this may be a step too far for most British voters, and politicians sizing up the potential pay-off might be excused for thinking it is not worth the aggravation.

Insurance to fund old age care

Age UK estimates that only 16 per cent of people aged over 85 will end up needing residential or nursing care, although this proportion may rise as more of us live longer. But for those who do need it, the cost can be eye-wateringly expensive: in 2013 the average weekly charge for residential care was £580, and £700 for nursing home care.[98]

We have seen that a relatively low-risk but high-cost expense like this is usually best covered by insurance. This is even more true for an expense that hits very late in life (for it becomes impossible for those who need the money to accumulate any more if their savings prove deficient, while those who do not need it have little opportunity to use what they have saved for some other fruitful purpose).

Under current arrangements in the UK, many people already save indirectly for their nursing home costs because elderly people who own their homes are obliged to draw down most of the capital to pay for their care and residential fees. Some commentators, including the Reform think tank, see little wrong with this.[99] Why shouldn't people be required to sell up their homes to pay for end-of-life care, rather than expecting taxpayers to foot the bill so they can pass on their wealth to their children?

But there is a clear unfairness in expecting those who have bought their homes to sell them and use up most of their assets before they can claim any state assistance, while those who have spent their lifetime earnings on other things qualify straight away for state financial support. It sounds like a reversal of the parable of the three talents – the less you have built up over your life, the better you get treated. This is certainly in breach of the instinctive sense of fairness discussed in Part I: it is right that everyone who needs care should get it, but it is unfair that people who have saved get penalised while those who have not get assisted (regardless of why they have no assets).

Rather than tackling this problem head-on, the Coalition government has come up with an unsatisfactory compromise which will increase government welfare spending without resolving the inequity. In future, individuals' lifetime care costs (but not the cost of board and lodging in care homes) will be capped at £75,000, and the state will pick up the tab for any excess.[100] But home owners will still have to meet most of the cost of care out of their own resources (normally by selling the family home), for assistance will only be offered once the elderly person's assets have been run down to £123,000.[101] This new scheme therefore exposes the taxpayer to increased claims while doing very little to solve the original inequity.

Compulsory old age care insurance would be a much better solution. Before the 2010 election, the Labour Party advocated a pooled-risk solution involving a compulsory levy on all deceased people's estates, but the Conservatives sought short-term electoral popularity by labelling the proposal a 'death tax'.[102] It would have been more constructive had they come up with a better, insurance-based proposal of their own.

Few people currently save or insure against the eventuality that they may need expensive care in their old age, so some sort of compulsory levy seems appropriate. Labour's idea for a tax might work, but some form of insurance would be preferable, for it offers a more efficient and equitable solution to the problem. Insurance could be offered by the government, or by private sector insurers with the government's role limited to external regulation.[103] Either way, premiums could be paid out of personal welfare accounts (financial institutions offering these accounts could package age-care insurance in with them). Everybody in employment would be required to insure themselves up to a certain level, but the choice of insurer and the comprehensiveness of cover beyond this basic level could be left up to individuals to decide for themselves.

Making the Transition

Economists tell us our National Insurance system no longer makes much sense. People who pay National Insurance contributions commonly get no additional benefit as a result, and those who do not pay are increasingly treated as if they did. Vast swathes of the British public have no idea what their contributions are funding, and many are under the misapprehension that their money is being put away for the future when it is actually being spent on existing benefit claimants and pensioners. National Insurance has, in all but name, become little more than a cumbersome second layer of income tax – except it is not applied to all incomes, it is opaque rather than transparent, and it costs millions of pounds to administer. Many economists believe these are compelling reasons for merging it with the income tax system.

Politicians, however, seem to have decided against such a course of action. The Chancellor of the Exchequer, George Osborne, wants income tax and National Insurance to be brought closer into alignment, but he has expressed his support for the principle that people should make contributions to fund their own pensions and benefits. Meanwhile, the Labour Party has begun talking about reinforcing the contributory principle as it applies to working-age benefits, floating the idea that larger payments might be made to people who have built up a long history of National Insurance contributions. After years of allowing the 'contributory principle' of National Insurance to erode, it seems that politicians have now begun (belatedly) to defend it, and even to look for ways of strengthening it, but few seem to have a clear plan for how this might be done.

If we want to keep both the economists and the politicians happy, it seems we need *both* to abolish National Insurance *and* to renew the contributory principle. This is not as contradictory as it sounds. As we saw in Part III, proposals have been kicking around the think-tank world for some years to replace some or all state pensions and benefits with self-funded alternatives based on savings and personal insurance. Going down this route could allow us to blend National Insurance into the income tax system as the economists recommend, while at the same time bolstering the principle that people should, whenever possible, accept responsibility for financing their own welfare needs.

Rather than contributing to a government welfare scheme, the idea is that people should contribute to their own, personal schemes, either by building up savings (to cover predictable income shortfalls like retirement), or by insuring against unpredictable but catastrophic risks (like the need for extended nursing home care in old age), or through some combination of the two. Younger people with insufficient funds might also borrow, replenishing their pots from future earnings (as they currently do to finance higher education fees).

These are not whimsical ideas. They are based on experience of real-world, highly successful schemes, such as those pioneered in Singapore and Chile. Indeed, influenced by these examples (and driven by the growing crisis of affordability in their conventional state welfare systems), many western countries, Britain included, have begun moving towards self-funded retirement pensions, and some have also extended the purpose of these personal savings funds to encompass other risks like temporary unemployment, sickness or parental leave. The foundations are therefore already in place on which we might develop a new system of personal welfare accounts.

The obvious objection to moving away from universal state provision towards more individualised funding options is that some poorer people may not be able to save and insure themselves sufficiently to cover their needs. But the statistics on tax/welfare churning in the existing social security system prove that, over a whole lifetime, most people can.

We saw in Part III that three-quarters of all the tax and National Insurance money spent by the UK government on the welfare state eventually goes back to the same people who contributed it in the first place. Only a quarter is redistributed between different people or households. This means that for most of us, the state pension and benefits system is already functioning more as an enforced savings and insurance scheme (delivering lifetime income smoothing) than as a redistributive support system (taking money from the affluent and channelling it to the needy).

It is true that not everybody will be able to cover their lifetime risks through their own funds, and for those who cannot, state assistance will still be required and should still be provided. But the challenge is to whittle away at that 74 per cent of state funding that is being churned while still redistributing the 26 per cent that is going to support the poorest lifetime income groups. If government reduced the scale of what it does for us using our own money, it could lower the tax burden leaving most of us with more cash to support ourselves and our families. We could then begin to take more responsibility for our own welfare without harming those who have to rely on state assistance.

Moving to a system of personal welfare accounts would be more efficient than our present system, and it would be fairer. It would be more efficient because we could splice together National Insurance and income tax (as the economists suggest), ending up with a single tax which is more transparent and less costly to administer. And because we would be using more of our own money to support ourselves, rather than dipping into a common pool, we would be less inclined to make unnecessary or fraudulent claims. The cost of providing for our welfare should therefore drop significantly.

A system of personal welfare accounts would also be fairer, for it embodies the basic, instinctive, ethical principle of proportionality. This principle that, whenever possible, you should give as well as take, has increasingly been overlooked and forgotten in our modern welfare system where the emphasis has almost exclusively come to be placed on the relief of need, regardless of its causes or circumstances.

We saw in Part I that our shared moral intuitions demand that those in need should be offered assistance, *and* that relief should be organised, managed and financed in a way that is fair to everyone, donors as well as recipients. A welfare system which fails to respect the ethic of proportionality will sooner or later sacrifice popular legitimacy as increasing numbers of people feel they are being 'taken for a ride' by undeserving claimants. It will also foster the spread of social irresponsibility as the idea takes hold that welfare is an unconditional right and that careless or reckless behaviour carries no costs. Both these developments are clear to see in Britain today.

The case for a move away from National Insurance towards a greater use of personal welfare accounts is therefore social as well as economic. Given the growing scale of state pension liabilities (at the last count, about four times the size of the National Debt), the economic case for reform is pressing and obvious, but the social arguments are no less important. Giving people more responsibility for looking after themselves is the indispensible condition for nurturing more responsible citizens.

So how do we do it? What would a system based on personal accounts look like and (just as important) how do we get from here to there?

We have seen in this report that Britain's social security system is already undergoing some radical transformations. The main non-contributory, working-age benefits are being replaced by a single, means-tested payment (the Universal Credit) which is being phased in between 2013 and 2017. The contributory state pension is being restructured in 2016 to absorb the additional second state pension, with opt-outs no longer allowed for those paying into private schemes. And employees who are not already members of an occupational or private pension scheme are being 'auto-enrolled' into new workplace pensions which will be fully operational by 2018 (although those who wish to opt out of these can do so). In addition, as already noted, the government hopes to bring National Insurance and income tax schedules into alignment, although there are no plans as yet to merge the two.

These are major changes which cannot now be reversed or changed (even if we wanted to) without huge disruption and expense. The task, therefore, is to graft the additional changes we need onto these reforms: a strategy of evolution, not revolution. Fortunately, we are already moving in the direction we want to go. Just eight more steps are needed to get there, and each follows on from the last.

Step 1. Wind up the National Insurance system

The National Insurance system, set up by Lloyd George before the First World War and reformed by Attlee's government in the wake of the Second, is no longer fit for purpose and should be wound up. This forms the starting point for all the other reforms that follow.

This report has elaborated at some length the problems with National Insurance and the reasons why many analysts now believe it should be integrated fully with income tax. National Insurance contributions do not accumulate in a fund, people are confused and misinformed about what their contributions are paying for, the costs of running two different systems are high, and (most important of all) the link between benefits and contributions has been broken. The contributory principle is crucially important, but in the modern National Insurance system, it is little more than a fiction.

Managing the integration of National Insurance into the tax system will be no simple task. A paper from the Institute of Fiscal Studies considers the practical obstacles in some detail.[1] They include the different definition and treatment of earnings, benefits in kind and work-related expenses in the National Insurance and income tax systems; their different periods of assessment of income (weekly versus yearly); their different units of assessment (tax is levied on the individual's income from all employments, while National Insurance is assessed separately for each job); the more generous treatment of the self-employed in the National Insurance system; the exemption from NICs of savings, investment and pension income; and differences in the way the two systems assess earnings of individuals over retirement age. There is also the problem that, if we abolish entitlement on the basis of National Insurance contributions, some other way will have to be found for determining eligibility for benefits.[2]

The IFS believes that, although some of these problems do pose difficulties, none is prohibitive.[3] It suggests the biggest obstacle is probably the reluctance of politicians to engage in a shake-up which will inevitably create losers as well as winners. But the government is now looking at how tax and National Insurance might better be harmonised, so even the political difficulties may not be insurmountable.

If National Insurance is scrapped, something has to be done about employers' as well as employees' contributions. The employee 12 per cent contribution would have to be added to the basic income tax rate of 20 per cent, creating a new basic rate of 32 per cent (perhaps with adjustments for older workers, the self-employed, people receiving income from savings and pensions, and others who currently enjoy more favourable treatment in the National Insurance system). The higher tax rate of 40 per cent would similarly rise to 42 per cent to take account of the 2 per cent NIC levied on earnings above the upper earnings limit. But what would happen to the 13.8 per cent employers' NICs?

One attractive suggestion is to do away with employers' contributions. This would reduce total government revenue by a bit more than four per cent, but it would make it cheaper to employ people. Those arguing for such a move claim it could generate another half a million jobs, and hence boost net income tax revenues in the long run.[4] Given the current problems with the public accounts, however, the Treasury seems unlikely to take such a risk.

Another option, canvassed by some economists, is that employer NICs could be added to the new income tax rates along with employee contributions, with employers required to raise wage levels by a corresponding amount. Since they are an indirect tax on the wages fund (for what employers pay in NICs cannot be paid in wages), why not come clean and levy workers directly? However, compelling as this economic logic may be, the political difficulties of raising the basic rate of income tax to 45.8 per cent are almost certainly too great for any government to risk doing it.

The third possibility is to retain employer NICs but turn them into a simple Payroll Tax, with the money going into general revenues in the same way as any other tax payments. This is the option favoured by the IFS, and it is probably the simplest and most plausible strategy from a political, as well as economic, point of view.

Whatever the eventual details of the transition, abolishing NICs as a separate tax immediately poses the question of how eligibility for retirement pensions and working-age benefits should be established in the absence of contributions. We shall consider the pension first, for as we have seen, it is the big ticket item in the National Insurance system, and it soaks up the lion's share of all the money that people currently pay in. Once pensions are sorted out, working-age benefits can be slotted in to the new system too.

Step 2. Establish entitlement to the new state pension through residency

The new state pension which is being introduced from 2016 is to be paid in full to everyone who has paid 35 years of National Insurance contributions. Those who have paid NICs for more years than this will get no credit for their over-payments; those who have paid for less will get less *pro rata*, unless they have fewer than ten years of contributions, in which case they will get nothing at all. People with reduced or no eligibility for the state pension, and with little or no other source of income, will still be able to apply for the means-tested, taxpayer-funded, Pension Credit.

If NICs were scrapped, new eligibility rules for the state pension would have to be introduced. We could substitute income tax payments records for NICs and keep the existing time periods as they are, although some annual threshold would have to be devised to determine how much tax somebody should have paid in a year to establish a full year's entitlement. This proposal would also require HMRC to retain complete income tax records over extended periods of time.

A simpler solution would be to determine eligibility by length of residency in the country. This is the strategy favoured by the IFS and most other groups arguing for abolition of NICs, and it is what happens in other countries (like Australia) which pay state pensions directly out of tax revenues. Residency of, say, ten years prior to reaching retirement age is probably an appropriate requirement. This would have the effect that most people drawing the state pension would have made some sort of tax contribution before retirement, even though this would no longer be the criterion by which their eligibility for the pension was determined. It would also have the advantage of being strictly gender-neutral.[5]

Giving every long-term resident a right to a state pension without a prior contributions requirement sounds like a recipe for a huge rise in government spending, but in reality it would be quite cheap. From 2016, about 90 per cent of retired people will qualify for the state pension under the existing rules (as we saw earlier in this report, many are 'deemed' to have made contributions, even when they haven't), so extending coverage to close to 100 per cent is not a big step.[6] Nor is this expensive, for under current rules, the ten per cent who do not qualify for the state pension will be able to apply for Pension Credit instead, and at its maximum, this will pay just one per cent less than the new, basic state pension will pay.

We may as well scrap the Pension Credit altogether and give all long-term residents the right to claim a basic state pension, for with Pension Credit, this is effectively what we will be doing anyway.

Step 3. Phase in a state pension means-test for new retirees

Scrapping NICs and establishing residency as the sole qualification for receipt of a state pension may not cost much more than the planned system will cost from 2016; but given the state of the public finances, and projections for the escalating cost of state pensions between now and the middle of this century, we should be looking to reduce the cost that future generations are going to be asked to bear.

That we are not currently taking this problem very seriously can be seen by the Coalition government's refusal even to withdraw or means-test costly but largely unnecessary privileges enjoyed by the over-60s such as the winter fuel allowance (annual cost: £2.1bn) and free bus travel (£1bn).[7] Politicians worry about antagonising the 'grey vote', for the elderly are not only outnumbering the young, they are also more electorally active.

The government has decided to raise the qualifying age for the state pension, and there are plans to peg this to average life expectancy. This should stabilise the size of the pensioner population, but it will not reduce the cost of giving them all pensions. Only means-testing will achieve that.

We have seen that means-testing the state pension could save £40bn or more per year once all existing NIC-based pension claims have passed through the system. This is a huge potential saving and it could substantially lower the tax burden on future cohorts of workers. Not surprisingly, many economists believe that means-testing is less a question of if than when.

The case for means-testing is not solely an economic one, however. It is, first and foremost, a principled one, for once we move from a contributions-based state pension to a tax-funded one, the justification for a universal state pension collapses.

When people pay contributions to establish a right to a pension, there is no justification for means-testing. Like any other insurance or savings plan, people who pay NICs must be paid out according to their earned entitlements, irrespective of whether they need the money, or how much they need. This is why any move to a means-tested pension will have to be phased in, so existing, earned entitlements are protected.[8]

But if the state pension is made non-contributory, and is financed instead from general tax revenues, people will cease to create entitlements through contributions. The state retirement pension will then look more like a working-age benefit such as the Universal Credit, paid on the basis of need. Just because you have paid taxes does not mean you should receive it. Indeed, fairness demands that a taxpayer-funded state pension should be means-tested. It is unconscionable that low-paid workers should be required to pay income tax so that people much better-off than they are can be given state pensions that they do not need.

Having said that, we must also acknowledge that there is a very strong argument against introducing even more means-testing into our welfare system. Means tests undermine work (or in the case of retirement pensions, savings) incentives by rewarding people who make no provision for themselves and penalising those who do. If the state pension is to be means-tested, this will inevitably increase the incentive for people to blow their savings and cash in their assets before they get to retirement age so they can qualify for the full pension from the government. This could prove costly, as well as being very unfair on those who do save.

The answer to this problem lies in a simple tweaking of the rules governing the new workplace pensions.

Step 4: Make workplace pensions compulsory

If the state pension is means-tested, saving in private retirement accounts has to be made compulsory to prevent deliberate dis-saving. Everyone who earns a significant income should be enrolled in a personal pension plan designed to generate an adequate retirement income by making regular contributions out of current earnings and converting funds into annuities on retirement.

We saw in Part III that compulsory retirement saving is now common in many other countries, but in Britain, we have stopped agonisingly short of it. While our new workplace pensions scheme will, when fully operational in 2018, require all employers to offer their workers membership of a portable pensions saving fund, and even to 'auto-enrol' them in it, it will not require their workers to remain in it.

The right of workers to opt out of workplace pensions (even if they have no other private pension plan) has its merits. It reflects a welcome liberal instinct on the part of the government (for although the policy of auto-enrolment tries to 'nudge' people to save, it stops short of imposing a paternalistic rule that we must save 'for our own good'). It also allows people to make their own judgements about the best long-term use of their own money (e.g. some may believe that starting a business, or buying property, will deliver better long-term returns than saving in a workplace pension to buy an annuity).

But if we are to reduce the financial burden on future generations of workers who will have to finance state pensions, mandatory saving is essential.

Step 5. Freeze current National Insurance entitlements and recognise them as government debt

Once National Insurance is scrapped, people will cease to build up any new entitlements to a state pension. But many people will already have made contributions up to that point, and these entitlements will still need to be honoured.

As we saw in Part III, these existing pension obligations are a sunk cost totalling £3.8 trillion at the last count. No matter what we do from now on, this money is going to have to be paid by future generations of taxpayers as and when past National Insurance contributors retire and draw on their entitlements. The only real question is how can these obligations best be met?

There appear to be two possibilities. One is to follow Chile's example and issue all those who have made National Insurance contributions in the past with bonds to the value of their current entitlements, indexed to inflation, and set to mature when they reach the statutory minimum retirement age. These bonds could be paid into people's workplace pension funds, and once cashed-in, the money would be used to buy annuities when they retire.

This option has the great advantage that it explicitly treats the government's pension obligations as part of the national debt, forcing politicians to address the problem of how the huge financial obligations we have built up in the past are going to be discharged. The disadvantage is that bonds have to be paid out as lump sums when they mature (i.e. as people reach retirement age), so the cost of paying people their pensions is front-loaded. Rather than spreading their payments over many years of their retirement, the whole lot is paid in one go at the start of it (although governments could roll over these debts by issuing new bonds to cover them).

It may be better simply to freeze people's NIC records on the day the system is wound up, index their existing state pension entitlement to take account of inflation, and then pay them this amount as a weekly or monthly pension from when they retire until they die. Under the proposals outlined in this report (and unlike Chile), the state pension will not disappear, but will simply be means-tested and therefore targeted. Existing entitlements could therefore easily be paid alongside means-tested pensions.

Whichever way existing entitlements are managed, it is important that they should be explicitly acknowledged by future governments as part of total public sector borrowing. Governments should be required to factor the cost of these pension entitlements into their calculations when setting their borrowing, taxing and spending plans.

Step 6. Boost personal retirement savings accounts

Even if participation in the new workplace pensions is made mandatory (step 4), minimum contributions have probably been set at too low a level to guarantee financial self-reliance in retirement.

Combining the employee's and employer's contribution, and adding the value of government tax relief, 11 per cent of salary will be paid into these funds. In Australia, where compulsory superannuation contributions are currently being raised from 9 per cent to 12 per cent, it is estimated that by mid-century (when the scheme fully matures), more than three-quarters of retirees will still have private pensions low enough to qualify them for a (full or part) means-tested government age pension on top.[9] While an 11 per cent contribution will make a significant difference, therefore, it seems that even if we means-test the UK state pension, it will still form the core component of many people's retirement income.

The problem with raising the 11 per cent workplace pension contribution level is obvious. Even lower-paid workers on basic rate tax are already losing 32 per cent of their wages in income tax and NICs, and their employers are paying another 13.8 per cent in NICs. The new pension will bump up the total, minimum employee deduction to 38.4 per cent, with another 16.8 per cent coming from their employers – a huge total deduction from the wage package of 55.2 per cent. How much more can be squeezed out of people's wages?

The answer has to be: we have reached the ceiling. Any future increase in workplace pension contributions must be funded by reducing the government's tax-take from employees, employers, or preferably both. With the current parlous state of the public finances, any such reduction seems a long way off. However, if the state pension is means-tested, substantial savings in government spending will gradually start to accrue. These savings should be ring-fenced from the start and fed back to the workforce in the form of tax savings.

Over the next few years, the aim should be to reduce employer Payroll Tax (the current employers' NIC) from 13.8 per cent to 12 per cent (switching the 1.8 per cent reduction into an enhanced employer contribution to workplace pensions), and at the same time to reduce the basic rate of income tax for employees from 32 per cent (the current 20 per cent basic rate plus 12 per cent NIC) to 30 per cent (switching the two per cent reduction into an enhanced employee contribution to the workplace pension). This would take the minimum total contribution into workplace pensions to almost 15 per cent, which is probably the minimum required. The government should commit itself to a clear timetable for managing this switch, based on the projected flow of revenue savings accruing from means-testing of the state pension.

There are also some one-off things the government could do to boost the asset levels of people's workplace pensions. The government is planning a 90 per cent privatisation of Royal Mail, which would raise £4bn.[10] And shares in the banks that were taken into public ownership at the time of the 2008 crash have also still to be sold back into the private sector. The state's 39 per cent share in Lloyds Banking Group is said to be worth around £17bn, and the much larger 81 per cent share in RBS is worth around £33bn. Both banks will be ready for partial or full re-privatisation from 2014.[11]

There is a strong case for saying that some of these shares (or some of the receipts from their sale) should be credited to people's workplace pension accounts. The Deputy Prime Minister has floated the idea that bank shares could be given away free to every member of the public, but this idea is both impractical and unfair.[12] Any free allocation of bank shares should be limited to people who are working and paying taxes, for it was taxpayers who bailed the banks out in the first place.

Current workers are going to have to foot the huge state pension bill in future years, even though they will forfeit the right to a universal state pension for themselves if and when the pension starts to be means-tested. It would therefore be fair and equitable if some of the shares from forthcoming privatisations were credited to their pension accounts. This could be done as a straight give-away, or on a deferred payment basis as recently proposed in a thoughtful paper by Policy Exchange.[13]

A proportion of future revenue from the sale of other state assets – such as auctions of mobile phone licences – and from taxes on the development of newly-discovered natural assets – such as gas and oil fracked from shale rock deposits – should also be set aside to boost people's pension accounts. Income from the North Sea oil and gas bonanza, as well as from the wave of 1980s privatisations, was frittered away on current spending by governments at the time. Any future revenue from assets like these should be ring-fenced and used to pay down government liabilities. Allocating part of these revenues to people's workplace pension funds is one of the best ways to accomplish this. By helping future retirees to enjoy higher private pensions, it reduces their reliance on the means-tested state pension, and this will reduce the burden on future generations of workers.

Step 7. Gradually extend the permitted uses of workplace pension funds to develop them into personal welfare accounts

Pensions are the core of the National Insurance system, but we also have to consider the future of working-age benefits once NICs are scrapped.

In the short-term, contributory benefits such as contribution-based JSA and ESA can be spliced into the non-contributory Universal Credit. We saw in Part I that nowadays there is precious little advantage in receiving a contributory benefit rather than its non-contributory equivalent – their cash value is exactly the same, and both are subject to activity conditions. Contributory benefits are not means-tested, but nor do they bring entitlement to other benefits, like free school meals, which people on non-contributory benefits can claim.

Abolition of National Insurance offers the opportunity to bring an end to this confusing and increasingly pointless distinction in the benefits system. Existing entitlement rules limit contributory benefits to those who have paid NICs over a preceding two-year period. Contributory working-age benefits could therefore be scrapped two years after NICs are ended without denying anybody a benefit to which they are entitled by virtue of the NICs they have paid.

This does not mean that people with strong employment records should then be treated in exactly the same way as those with weak or non-existent records. Quite the reverse. For at the same time as contributory benefits are scrapped, the rules governing the use of workplace pension funds should be changed to allow people to access a proportion of their funds (or in specified cases to borrow against them) to cover relatively short periods of unemployment. This would then exempt people who have been working and building up savings from the activity conditions which should be applied to those claiming state benefits (see Step 8, below).

This expansion in the role of workplace accounts should probably be limited in the first instance to funding short spells of unemployment. As explained in Part III, there would need to be a clear time limit (probably six months) on this use of personal funds to ensure that future pensions are not put at risk. The monthly sums drawn from accounts should also be restricted so that they do not exceed the amount that would have been paid by the benefits system.

With these rules in place, a single worker on the average wage who has been paying into a workplace account for just two years, and who then experiences a six-month period of unemployment, would deplete his or her account by just under one-third if they drew an income from their account rather than claiming Universal Credit. It would then take them less than eight months to replenish their account once they got back into employment and resumed their regular contributions.[14]

Further expansion in the purposes to which these accounts might be put should occur gradually. The longer accounts are in existence, the more money they will contain, the more the contributions rate will have a chance to rise as income tax rates fall (step 6), and the more people will grow accustomed to the idea of using their own funds to cover temporary interruptions in their earnings. In Singapore and Chile, personal accounts began purely as retirement saving vehicles and expanded later. The same should happen here. Given time, these accounts could be developed to cover people's incomes in periods of short-term sickness, parental leave to care for children, and perhaps certain aspects of their health care expenditure. But not all of this can or should be attempted at once.

Having said that, two additional uses of personal accounts should be considered as priorities. One is that existing and future student loans should be integrated into them (i.e. the debt should count against the account, and the regular 11 per cent mandated contributions should go to paying it off). The other is that detailed proposals should be brought forward for including basic insurance against old-age care costs as a compulsory element of all personal accounts.

Step 8. Apply activity conditions to receipt of working-age benefits

The final piece of the jigsaw relates to the provision of working-age benefits. Unconditional support for people who cannot be expected to work (basically, severely disabled people and single parents with infant children under one year) should continue, but for those who are capable of working full- or part-time, appropriate work-based activity conditions should be attached to any and every receipt of state benefits.

This step is essential, not only to demarcate receipt of taxpayer-funded benefits from reliance on personal welfare accounts (where no activity conditions should apply), but also to fulfil the fairness principle that those claiming state benefits should be no better off than the lowest-paid worker. We saw in Part I that this principle applies, not only to the money they receive, but also to the control they have over their own *time*.

Many on the left think activity conditions are only justified if they improve the situation of claimants, but just because workfare schemes may offer little of advantage to those who participate in them does not mean they serve no useful purpose. They strengthen work incentives by shifting the calculus of advantage as between working and claiming, and they create greater fairness by equivalising the treatment of those on benefits with those in employment. If someone who is capable of working claims state benefits, they should be willing to give up their time, just as the taxpayers who are supporting them have to give up theirs.

◆ ◆ ◆ ◆ ◆

The eight proposals outlined above may appear radical, but they represent little more than a re-application of the key ideas and principles which Beveridge hoped to implement in the 1940s. He wanted to establish a system of social protection based on the two equally important moral imperatives of help for those in need, and fairness grounded in the contributory principle. These are the same two ethical principles on which these eight recommendations have been based.

Beveridge provided for the relief of need with a tax-funded, means-tested, conditional National Assistance safety net. He then tried to ensure fairness (proportionality) with a contributory National Insurance system in which everyone paid the same and established the same entitlements. But over the last 70 years, the contributory principle at the heart of his National Insurance system has withered, with the result that fairness has atrophied. The social security system in Britain today has a one-eyed focus on the relief of need and has largely forgotten about the importance of fairness.

Following these eight recommendations, Beveridge's twin pillars – a taxpayer-funded safety net involving limited income redistribution to assist those in need, coupled with a system of income-smoothing based on compulsory contributions to maximise lifetime self-reliance – can be reinstated.

◆ In place of needs-based National Assistance, we now have the Universal Credit – a tax-funded, means-tested benefit for working-age people. Beveridge thought it imperative that people in receipt of taxpayer-funded assistance like this should not enjoy more desirable circumstances than those experienced by people who contribute to their own support. Only by applying rigorous activity conditions to the receipt of Universal Credit can this concern be met.

◆ In place of National Insurance, which has all but collapsed as a system delivering genuine, contributions-based self-reliance, this report has advocated the development of compulsory personal welfare accounts, based on the new workplace pensions scheme. Financed by regular contributions, and offering pension and working-age income replacement as of right, these accounts can fulfil the promise of Beveridge's original plan for National Insurance. The crucial difference is that contributions remain under the control of contributors themselves in a system of personal welfare accounts, and are therefore secure against the predations of future governments.

William Beveridge's National Insurance system was conceived as an ethical system, but it developed over the space of 70 years into a giant, state-sponsored Ponzi scheme in which each generation has robbed the one coming up behind it. With the state pension debt now approaching four trillion pounds, the time has come to wind up this deceitful and immoral game of generational pass-the-parcel.

But as we dismantle the National Insurance system, the contributory principle at the heart of Beveridge's thinking can and must be salvaged. In this report, we have seen how personal welfare accounts offer the best opportunity for realising Beveridge's flawed but deeply moral plan for Britain.

Notes

Introduction

1   Patrick Nolan, Lauren Thorpe, Kimberley Trewhitt, *Entitlement Reform*, London: Reform, November 2012, p.12

Part 1: Fairness and the Contributory Principle

1   *Report of the Inter-Departmental Committee on Social Insurance and Allied Services*, Macmillan, 1942

2   James Bartholomew, *The welfare state we're in*, London: Politico's, 2004, p.56

3   BBC archive, 'Sir William Beveridge announcement', 2 December 1942, http://www.bbc.co.uk/archive/nhs/5139.shtml

4   One of the most famous instances of this was probably Aneurin Bevan's notorious comment that Tories are 'lower than vermin'. I have discussed other examples of left-wing moral hubris in Peter Saunders, *Remoralising the welfare state* (Sydney: Centre for Independent Studies, 2013), on which much of this section of this paper is based.

5   Jonathon Haidt, *The Righteous Mind*, Allen Lane, 2012

6   Part of Haidt's motivation for writing the book was to encourage greater dialogue across these divides. As he puts it: 'Each team is composed of good people who have something important to say' (Haidt, p.313). He complains about the political polarisation in modern America and wants us all to endorse the socialist case for more regulation, the classical liberal case for free markets, and the conservative case for defending cultural homogeneity.

7   Not everybody, of course, recognises this moral imperative. Those who don't are generally labelled as psychopaths. Haidt accepts that, as we grow up, we may become more concerned to demonstrate our goodness to others than to actually be good. But this craving to influence the way we are perceived by others is again a product of our evolution. If we can make others believe (wrongly) that we are observing the shared moral rules, we will enjoy the same benefits of co-operation as if we really were behaving correctly.

8   Haidt points out that religious and political movements may deliberately target these instinctive care triggers to elicit our emotional commitment to one cause rather than another. The things that trigger kindness and compassion thus vary over time and across places, and they

are to some extent learned or even manipulated.

9   Robert Axelrod, *The Evolution of Cooperation*, New York: Basic Books, 1984, p. 54. Tit-for-tat requires certain conditions to be fulfilled if it is to be the most successful strategy. In particular, participants must be able to recognise each other and recall their past interactions in order to know how to respond, and they must value the outcomes of future interactions as well as the immediate outcome of their present one.

10   Haidt, p.136

11   Haidt, p.180

12   Axelrod makes a similar point, noting that penalising defectors 'helps to police the entire community by punishing those who try to be exploitative' (*The Evolution of Cooperation*, p.139). Everyone benefits as a result.

13   Libertarians (or classical liberals) are also lop-sided in their moral values, according to Haidt, strongly emphasising the 'liberty' and 'proportionality' foundations at the expense of the other four.

14   Haidt, p.184

15   Suzanne Hall, *21st century welfare*, London: Ipsos MORI Social Research Institute, 2012, p.12

16   http://www.comres.co.uk/polls/BBC_Welfare_Poll_November2012. pdf, Table 11

17   Neil O'Brien, 'Just Desserts? Attitudes to Fairness, Poverty and Welfare Reform', Policy Exchange *Research Note*, April 2011

18   Hall, *21st century welfare* , p.13

19   Neil O'Brien, 'Just Desserts?, p.2

20   *The Sunday Times*, 3 October 2010

21   Ipsos MORI, *Employment, welfare, skills and the economy: public perceptions and expectations*, August 2010

22   'The first and most essential of all conditions is that the situation of the individual relieved should not be made really or apparently so eligible as the situation of the independent labourer of the lowest class', Poor Law Commissioners' report, 1834, quoted by J. Brown, *Victims or Villains? Social Security Benefits in Unemployment* , Policy Studies Institute, 1990, p.3

23   *BBC Radio 4 Welfare Poll*, Table 10. Just nine per cent disagreed. http://www.comres.co.uk/polls/BBC_Welfare_Poll_November2012.pdf

24   Derek Fraser, *The Evolution of the British Welfare State*, MacMillan, 1973, p.143

25   *Big Society: What do we know?* IPSOS-Mori Social Research Institute Briefing Pack, 2010

26   YouGov survey for *The Daily Telegraph*, 23-25 July 2008. For

an example of the opposition to such a policy, see Michael Spencer, Jordana Muroff, Jorge Delva, 'Conditional welfare: A family social work perspective on mandatory drug testing', *Journal of Family Social Work*, vol.4, 2000, 3-14

Part II: The Corrosion of National Insurance

1   Both Jobseeker's Allowance and Employment & Support Allowance take two forms, depending on whether recipients have a National Insurance contributions record. The 'income-based' payments are for those who do not. For details of the reform, see: https://www.gov.uk/government/policies/simplifying-the-welfare-system-and-making-sure-work-pays/supporting-pages/introducing-universal-credit

2   *BBC Radio 4 Welfare Poll*, ComRes, November 2012, Table 2. http://www.comres.co.uk/polls/BBC_Welfare_Poll_November2012.pdf

3   'Most back benefits reform', *Sunday Times*, 7 April 2013

4   Among social classes C2, D and E, agreement with the proposition that half or more claimants were scrounging rises to close to 50 per cent. Interestingly, 46 per cent of those living on welfare benefits also believed that more than half of all claimants are 'scrounging'. *BBC Radio 4 Welfare Poll*, Table 2

5   David Green, *Reinventing Civil Society*, London: Institute of Economic Affairs, 1993. According to James Bartholomew, some 12 million people (workers and their dependents) were covered by the new state system of National Insurance introduced in 1911, but 10 million of these were already insured through friendly societies or trade unions (*The welfare state we're in*, p.51).

6   Fraser, *The Evolution of the British Welfare State*, p.155. Other family members were excluded from health cover. The involvement of approved societies in the provision of health cover continued until the establishment of the NHS in 1948.

7   Fraser, *The Evolution of the British Welfare State*, p.161

8   Fraser, *The Evolution of the British Welfare State*, p.150

9   A time limit of 26 weeks was reintroduced by the National Government in its crisis measures of 1931. The value of insured benefits was also cut at this time by ten per cent, and the transitional payment was tightly means tested and administered by new Public Assistance Committees.

10   Beveridge letter to Churchill, February 1930, quoted in Fraser, *The Evolution of the British Welfare State*, p.177

11   Brown, *Victims or Villains?*, p.18

12   A lower married women's rate continued (as an option) right up to 1977. Women who chose to pay the reduced rate lost any pension

entitlement.

13   Fraser, *The Evolution of the British Welfare State*, p.200

14   '...benefit in return for contributions, rather than free allowances from the State, is what the people of Britain desire. This desire is shown both by the established popularity of compulsory insurance, and by the phenomenal growth of voluntary insurance against sickness, against death and for endowment, and most recently for hospital treatment. It is shown in another way by the strength of popular objection to any kind of means test. This objection springs not so much from a desire to get everything for nothing, as from resentment at a provision which appears to penalise what people have come to regard as the duty and pleasure of thrift, of putting pennies away for a rainy day. Management of one's income is an essential element of a citizen's freedom. Payment of a substantial part of the cost of benefit as a contribution irrespective of the means of the contributor is the firm basis of a claim to benefit irrespective of means.' *Report on Social Insurance and Allied Services* (Cmnd 6404), 1942, para 21

15   BBC archive, 'Sir William Beveridge announcement', 2 December 1942, http://www.bbc.co.uk/archive/nhs/5139.shtml

16   Beveridge calculated that his scheme could remain in balance with unemployment as high as eight per cent (see Brown, *Victims or Villains?* chapter 2).

17   *Report on Social Insurance and Allied Services*, para 369

18   Beveridge wanted all insured benefits to be paid indefinitely, without time limits, but in the case of unemployment he accepted that some sort of work or training should be required of claimants after six months to prevent 'habituation to idleness' and to 'unmask' those who were working in the black economy while claiming benefits (see Brown, *Victims or Villains?*, p.26).

19   *The Contributory Principle*, House of Commons Select Committee on Social Security, 5th Report, June 2000, section 2.4

20   Antoine Bozio, Rowena Crawford and Gemma Tetlow, *The history of state pensions in the UK: 1948 to 2010*, Institute for Fiscal Studies, 2010, p.8

21   Ipsos-MORI reports that many Britons 'have little sense that the money that they pay via National Insurance Contributions (NICs) and through general taxation is being used to fund public services now. Rather, they assume that their contributions are being saved for their own use in the future' (Hall, *21st century welfare*, p.30). See also the results of focus group research in Bruce Stafford, *National Insurance and the contributory principle*, Dept of Social Security, 1998

22   A Ponzi scheme (named after American fraudster, Charles Ponzi)

defrauds investors by offering them huge gains which are financed out of later investors' money. Also known as a 'pyramid scheme', the bigger it gets, the faster it runs out of money.

23 Quoted by Philip Johnston, 'The pensions revolution arriving by stealth', *Daily Telegraph*, 25 September 2012

24 Brown, *Victims or Villains?* p.38. This discretionary 'extended benefit', only ever taken by four per cent of claimants, was ended in 1953 when provision for 'additional days' was extended to 19 months

25 Brown, *Victims or Villains?* pp.40 and 55

26 Brown, *Victims or Villains?* tables 3.3 and 3.6

27 Matthew Oakley and Peter Saunders, *No Rights Without Responsibility*, London: Policy Exchange, 2011

28 Nicholas Boys-Smith, *Reforming Welfare*, London: Reform, October 2006, p.14

29 Nolan *et al.*, *Entitlement Reform*, p.59, gives a figure of 15.8 per cent for 2011. David Brindle ('Private health insurance takes a dive', *The Guardian*, 19 July 2010) puts the figure somewhat lower at under 12 per cent. In *The Times*, Andrew Clark ('Economic ills prove contagious for private healthcare system', 16 July 2013) estimates just 10.8 per cent, corresponding to 6.9 million people in 2012.

30 Francis Fukuyama, *The Great Disruption*, Simon & Schuster, 1999

31 *The Contributory Principle*, House of Commons Select Committee on Social Security, sections 2.5-2.7

32 Beveridge proposed that married women should have a right to maternity benefit and widows/old age pension by virtue of their husbands' contributions. Until 1978, married women who worked had the right to opt out of unemployment benefit in return for lower NI contributions, the reasoning being that their husband – the 'principal wage earner' – could support them, and about three-quarters of them exercised this option. Today, all women workers pay the same contributions as men and receive the same level of benefits. Spouses who have earned no entitlement of their own through employment are entitled to 60 per cent of the pension rights earned by their partner's contributions and, if widowed, they get their former spouse's full entitlement. This applies only to couples who are married or in civil partnerships.

33 For details, see Peter Saunders, *Reforming the UK Family Tax and Benefits System*, London: Policy Exchange, 2009.

34 John Hills, *Inclusion or Insurance? National Insurance and the future of the contributory principle*, Centre for Analysis of Social Exclusion Paper 68, LSE, May 2003, Table 1

35 Bozio et al, *The History of State Pensions in the UK*, p.9. Repeated

experiences of governments defaulting on their promises have almost certainly eroded public trust in governments. Saving and insuring through personal welfare funds under our own control removes the need to rely on the dubious probity of politicians.

36   The second state pension was more generous to low earners and groups like carers and the long-term ill or disabled with fractured NI contributions records.

37   Details in Bozio *et al.*, *The History of State Pensions* section 4.2

38   The 2007 Pensions Act legislated to transform the earnings-related Second State Pension into a flat-rate pension by the 2030s (it also ended the right of workers in defined pension schemes to opt out). See DWP, *A State Pension for the 21st Century* Cm 8053, 2011, sections 40-44. This legislation has since been superseded by the Coalition's reform of the basic state pension which will from 2016 combine the original pension and the second pension into a single, flat-rate payment (discussed below).

39   Initially, pensioners with inadequate incomes could claim National Assistance. This was replaced in 1966 by Supplementary Benefit, then by Income Support, then the short-lived Minimum Income Guarantee, and from 2003, the Pension Credit. Details in Bozio *et al.*, *The History of State Pensions*, chapter 6

40   DWP, *A State Pension for the 21st Century*, p.21. In many cases, a failure to claim probably reflects the small size of the top-up payment which retired people with some other source of income might expect to receive.

41   Bozio *et al.*, *The History of State Pensions in the UK*, p.10

42   DWP, *The Single Tier Pension: A simple foundation for saving*, Dept of Work & Pensions, Cm 8528, January 2013. People who have been paying a lower rate of NICs because they belong to an occupational pension scheme and have opted out of the state second pension will receive a lower amount to reflect this.

43   There is a minimum qualifying period of ten years.

44   Public opinion is evenly divided on whether benefits should be graduated according to tax paid (as against NI contributions). A 2012 BBC Radio 4 welfare survey asked if 'people who have paid more in taxes should receive larger benefit payments'. 47 per cent thought they should, 41 per cent disagreed. http://www.comres.co.uk/polls/BBC_Welfare_Poll_November2012.pdf, Table 9

45   DWP, *The Single-tier Pension*, para 14; Hilary Osborne, 'Single tier pension Q&A', *The Guardian*, 14 January 2013

46   According to David Martin, about 30 per cent of women have sufficient NICs to qualify for a full state pension, compared with 85 per cent of men. *Abolish NICs*, Centre for Policy Studies, 2010, p.19

47   DWP, *A State Pension for the 21st Century*, p.33

48   DWP, *The Single-tier Pension*, p.25

49   I have discussed this assumption that equal outcomes are the overriding criterion of fairness in Peter Saunders, *The Rise of the Equalities Industry*, London: Civitas, 2011. Women on average earn less than men mainly because they follow different careers and take career breaks, not because they encounter 'glass ceilings'. When selecting careers, men tend to emphasise remuneration more than women do. Women are generally more concerned about job satisfaction and are more drawn to the public sector.

50   Paul Johnson, 'The pensions bill has policy lessons for us all', *The Guardian*, 27 January 2013

51   'It is confirmation of the end of any serious link between contributions into our supposed social insurance system and benefits received' (Johnson, 'The pensions bill has policy lessons for us all').

52   Bruce Stafford, *National Insurance and the Contributory Principle*, p.41

53   See Citizens Advice Bureau, http://www.adviceguide.org.uk/england/benefits_e/benefits_benefits_in_work_or_looking_for_work_ew/benefits_for_people_looking_for_work.htm#jobseekers_allowance_and_sanctions

54   David Martin, *Abolish NICs*, p.13

55   'The Jobseeker's Allowance combines the administration of means-tested and insured benefits, which means that as far as claimants are concerned it may be of no significance whether their entitlement derives from past contributions or not... The blurring of the boundaries between social assistance and social insurance undermines the basis of social insurance benefit as an entitlement based on contributions' (Angus Erskine, 'The withering of social insurance in Britain', in Jochen Clasen, [ed.], *Social Insurance in Europe*, Policy Press, 1997, p.144).

56   The others are New Zealand, Australia and Ireland (see Immervoll, 'Minimum income benefits in OECD countries', Table 4).

57   Labour's welfare spokesperson, Liam Byrne, is said to be developing proposals to pay higher benefits to those with long contributions records. See his article 'Why Conservative benefit cuts won't get Britain working', *The Observer*, 7 April 2013 – although it is unclear how this could be afforded without reducing the value of non-contributory benefits, which the Labour Party seems unlikely to countenance.

58   Peter Saunders, *Reforming the UK Family Tax and Benefits System*, London: Policy Exchange, 2009

59   HM Treasury, *Tax credits: Improving delivery and choice*, 2008; Peter Saunders, *Reforming the UK Family Tax and Benefits System*

60   Cathy Corrie and Patrick Nolan, 'Seismic shifts in the welfare state', *Reform Ideas* No.4, London: Reform, May 2013

61   Paul Johnson, 'It's time to bin the last vestige of Beveridge', *The Independent*, 2 December 2012. Johnson concludes: 'We need to recognise the contributory principle for what it has become – a fiction.'

62   Universal Credit is being introduced in selected areas between April and October 2013 to test it out. From October 2013, all new claimants, and those whose circumstances change, will go onto the new payment, and from April 2014, the new system is being rolled out over a three-year period for everyone else.

63   The aim of the new system is to ensure that claimants will always be better off if they increase their hours of work. But as a means-tested benefit, there will still be an income taper, so as you start to earn more, your benefit will reduce.

64   Bozio *et al.*, *The History of State Pensions in the UK*, pp.18-21 and Appendix B. From 2010, Home Responsibilities Protection has been made more generous for those with no or limited work records by treating child-rearing time as NI qualifying years (rather than reducing the number of years of contributions required). Those who accumulate many years of HRP but few years of earnings will now receive much bigger pensions than before.

65   Rory Meakin, *Abolish National Insurance*, London: Taxpayers' Alliance, 2011, p.11

66   The 2013 White Paper estimates that the proportion of people of retirement age claiming Pension Credit will fall to about 20 per cent by 2030, and to 10 per cent after that. DWP *The Single-tier Pension*, para 16

67   A. Erskine and J. Clasen, 'Social insurance in Europe – adapting to change', in J. Clasen (ed.) *Social Insurance in Europe*, Policy Press, 1997, p.250

68   The Taxpayers' Alliance is one exception: 'It is not fair on ordinary taxpayers that the unemployed and those on approved training courses are awarded credits and gain the same entitlement as those who are working' (Meakin, *Abolish National Insurance*, p.31).

69   John Hills, *Inclusion or Insurance?*, p.11

70   *The Contributory Principle*, House of Commons Select Committee on Social Security, 5th Report, June 2000, section 3.4

71   In 2010-11, retired people in receipt of state money were still relying mainly on a contributory benefit (the state pension) – only 22 per cent of the cash benefits going to retired families were non-contributory, compared with 74 per cent of the money going to working-age families. Cathy Corrie and Patrick Nolan, 'Seismic shifts in the welfare state', Table 4

72   David Martin, *Abolish NICs*, p.16. Figures provided by Martin indicate that in 2008-09, the National Insurance Fund received £78bn in NICs (this excludes NI revenues that went to the NHS). It paid out £70bn, of which £61bn (87 per cent) was for pensions. IFS figures (quoted by Antony Seely, *National Insurance Contributions: An introduction*, House of Commons Library, 2012, pp.3-4) show that real expenditure on contributory benefits increased from £42bn to £72bn (a 73 per cent rise) in the thirty years from1979, mainly due to the growing cost of the state pension. But during the same period, real spending on tax-funded, means-tested benefits increased from £11bn in 1979 to £74bn in 2010 (an increase of 580 per cent), much of it fuelled by the growth of tax credits.

73   David Martin, *Abolish NICs*, p.1

74   In 2010/11, the government raised £97bn from NICs compared with £150bn from income tax, £84bn from VAT, and £42bn from corporation tax - Antony Seely, *National Insurance contributions: An introduction* House of Commons Library, 2012, p.2.

75   Stuart Adam & Glen Loutzenhiser, 'Integrating Income Tax and National Insurance: An interim report', Institute for Fiscal Studies, *Working Paper* 21/07, 2007

76   A Taxpayers' Alliance report suggests that this damages labour relations, for employees do not realise the true level of their direct and indirect remuneration (Rory Meakin, *How to Abolish National Insurance*) London: Taxpayers' Alliance, 2012, p.7

77   Bruce Stafford, *National Insurance and the Contributory Principle*, p.16

78   Seely, *National Insurance Contributions: An introduction*, House of Commons Library, 2012, p.11

79   James Mirrlees and others, *Tax by design*, Institute for Fiscal Studies, 2011, p.128. This rise was unnecessary given that the NI fund was in surplus at the time.

80   John Hills, *Inclusion or insurance?*, pp.2-3. Focus group research confirms a widespread misconception that NICs fund the NHS (Stafford, *National Insurance and the Contributory Principle*, p.19). In fact, of the £98 billion raised by NICs in 2011, only £20bn went to the NHS (Antony Seely, *National Insurance Contributions: An introduction*, House of Commons Library, 2012, p.3). The NHS is, overwhelmingly, paid for out of general taxation, and access to free health care has never depended on NI contributions. It is true that when the Blair government raised the rate of Class I employee contributions from 11 per cent to 12 per cent, it claimed the extra revenue was needed to fund an increase in NHS spending, but in reality this money was interchangeable with tax revenues. As David

Martin explains: 'The Government can plan to increase expenditure on anything it wishes. If it then increases NICs to pay more to hospitals, the residue of expenditure that it needs to fund hospitals from general taxation is reduced, so that the Government thereby obtains the funds that it needs to release for the other planned expenditure.' (*Abolish NICs* p.10-11)

81   Stuart Adam & Glen Loutzenhiser, 'Integrating Income Tax and National Insurance: An interim report', p.14

82   However, the government estimated in 2007 that harmonising the NI and income tax collection rules (e.g. by moving to annual rather than weekly assessment of income for NICs) would save employers less than five per cent of their total payroll tax operation costs. It pointed out that computerisation has made it much easier to handle the two different deductions than it used to be (Seely, *National Insurance contributions: An introduction*, House of Commons Library, 2012, p.21).

83   IFS research in the mid-nineties estimated compliance costs per employee at £288 p.a. for employers with 1-4 employees, but only £5 p.a. for those with more than 5,000 employees (Stuart Adam & Glen Loutzenhiser 'Integrating Income Tax and National Insurance: An interim report', p.16). The Adam Smith Institute has argued for abolition of the employer's national insurance contribution for small and medium-sized businesses, saying this would save business almost £150m in compliance costs and lead directly to 500,000 more people being employed. Such a move would cost £18.5bn in lost revenue, but the Institute claims this would be recouped in three years through enhanced income tax receipts (Vuk Vukovic, 'Unburdening Enterprise', *Briefing Paper*, Adam Smith Institute, 2012).

84   This is the amount HMRC charges the National Insurance Fund for collecting NICs (Meakin, *Abolish National Insurance*, p.16).

85   Discussed in Brown, *Victims or Villains?*, p.155

86   Mirrlees and others, *Tax by Design*. Also Stuart Adam & Glen Loutzenhiser ,'Integrating Income Tax and National Insurance: An interim report'.

87   Mirrlees and others, *Tax by Design*

88   Stuart Adam & Glen Loutzenhiser, 'Integrating Income Tax and National Insurance: An interim report', p.3

89   Cited in Stuart Adam & Glen Loutzenhiser, 'Integrating Income Tax and National Insurance: An interim report', p.11

90   Rory Meakin, *How to Abolish National Insurance*, Taxpayers' Alliance 2012, Appendix C

91   Allister Heath, *The Single Income Tax: Summary of the 2020 Tax*

Commission Final Report, Taxpayers' Alliance & Institute of Directors, 2012. Also Meakin, *How to Abolish National Insurance*

92   Patrick Nolan, Lauren Thorpe and Kimberley Trewhitt, *Entitlement Reform*, chapter 6

93   David Martin, *Abolish NICs*

94   See for example Andrew Grice, 'Osborne's secret plan to raise tax and scrap national insurance', *The Independent*, 17 March 2011

95   Quoted in Seely, *National Insurance Contributions: An introduction*, House of Commons Library, 2012, p.28

96   'The problems associated with shifting to an entirely employee-based...tax look quite large [and] may not be worth attempting. Moreover it is probably too much to expect politicians seeking election to argue for the outright replacement of a major tax "on businesses" with an equivalent tax "on employees"' (Stuart Adam & Glen Loutzenhiser, 'Integrating Income Tax and National Insurance: An interim report', p.26).

97   John Hills, *Inclusion or insurance?*, p.13

98   For a detailed discussion of these problems, see Stuart Adam & Glen Loutzenhiser, 'Integrating Income Tax and National Insurance: An interim report', Section IV

99   David Martin, *Abolish NICs*, p.16

100   The Australian federal government introduced a national, tax-funded, means-tested age pension in 1909 which covered one-third of the retired population (before that, the New South Wales and Victoria state governments ran similar schemes). Although social insurance schemes were drafted in federal bills in 1928 and 1938, the switch was never made, and when benefits for working-age people were introduced in the 1940s, they too were non-contributory and financed from general taxation (Michael Jones, *The Australian Welfare State*, 4th edn, Allen & Unwin, 1996, chapter 2; Peter Whiteford and David Stanton, *Targeting, Adequacy and Incentives*, Paper to 9th International Research Seminar on Issues in Social Security, Sweden:Sigtuna, June 2002). Today, 55 per cent of retired Australians receive a full age pension, and another 25 per cent get a part pension (Stephen Kirchner, *Compulsory Super at 20*, Sydney: Centre for Independent Studies Policy Monograph 132, 2012, p.16). Continental European countries like Germany, France and Italy have strong social insurance systems and pensions are paid to all who contribute to them. However, the principle of social insurance in these countries is weakening as the same factors that undermined NI in Britain (growth of temporary working and decline of marriage) leave increasing numbers of people without cover (Angus Erskine & Jochen Clasen,

'Social insurance in Europe – adapting to change?', p.248).

101   When Chile moved from a pay-as-you-go state pension scheme to a system of personal savings accounts, it issued 'recognition bonds' yielding four per cent annual interest which were credited to people's personal retirement accounts at the point of retirement (Karl Bordern, 'How Chile broke the pensions chain letter', in Eamonn Butler, Mukul Asher and Karl Bordern, *Singapore versus Chile: Competing models for welfare reform*, London: Adam Smith Institute, 1996). Given that the UK would not be terminating the state pension, but only means-testing it, there would no need to follow this example; the pensions authority (DWP) could simply pay the pre-existing contributory component while also administering means-tested pensions. Issuing bonds would, however, have the advantage of making the existing implicit government debt explicit (see Barr, *The Welfare State as Piggy-Bank*, Oxford University Press, 2001, p.120).

102   For example, somebody who has seven years of NICs at the point when the existing system is terminated has already established an entitlement to 20 per cent of the full state pension (seven out of 35 years of contributions). On retirement, this 20 per cent entitlement would be honoured (in the form of weekly pension payments, or as a one-off payment of a mature bond which could purchase an annuity), irrespective of their financial circumstances. If they have no other income (including income from a partner), their 20 per cent earned pension entitlement would be made up to a full pension as a result of the means test. If, on the other hand, they have built up pension rights in a private or occupational scheme, and/or their household income from other sources takes them above the means-test limit, they would still receive the 20 per cent state pension to which their earlier NICs had entitled them, but nothing else on top.

103   Kirchner, *Compulsory Super at 20,* pp.16-17

104   Compulsory superannuation was set up in 1992 with employers contributing three per cent of employee earnings, rising to nine per cent by 2002 (Whiteford and Stanton, *Targeting, adequacy and incentives*, p.9). Contributions are entirely paid by employers, but this is typically recognised as part of the overall wage package. By the time the Australian superannuation system matures, only 36 per cent of retirees will qualify for the full, means-tested state pension (although another 40 per cent will get a fraction of it), for most will have at least some income from their personal super fund which they have been required by law to build up in the course of their working lives (Kirchner, *Compulsory Super at 20*, p.17). I shall discuss the issues raised by compulsory saving at more

length in Section III.

105   David Willetts, *The Pinch: How the baby boomers took their children's future, and why they should give it back*, London: Atlantic Books, 2010

106   Karl Bordern, 'How Chile broke the pensions chain letter', in Eamonn Butler, Mukul Ashaer and Karl Borden, *Singapore versus Chile*, London: Adam Smith Institute, 1996

107   Office for National Statistics estimates, reported in 'Barometer', *The Spectator*, 15 June 2013

108   Tim Ross, 'Ageing population pushes welfare bill to crisis point', *Daily Telegraph*, 25 July 2013

109   I discuss this further in the conclusion to this report, where I summarise my reform recommendations.

110   Peter Saunders, *A Nation of Home Owners*, Unwin Hyman, 1990

111   Alternatively, if the value of the domestic home were to be included in the means-test for the state pension (as some have suggested), the cost of the state pension borne by the working population would be dramatically lowered. The think-tank Reform points out that retired people in Britain currently own housing assets worth £907bn, and it suggests that in future, families should be willing to draw on some of this equity to help fund their retirement incomes, e.g. through greater use of equity release schemes (Patrick Nolan, Lauren Thorpe and Kimberley Trewhitt, *Entitlement Reform*, p.20).

112   Barr, *The welfare state as piggy bank*, p.121

113   Karl Bordern, 'How Chile broke the pensions chain letter'

Part III: Rescuing the Contributory Principle

1   Ryan Bourne, 'The progressivity of UK taxes and transfers', Statistical Factsheet 11, London: Centre for Policy Studies, October 2012

2   The 20 per cent marginal rate of income tax rises to 40 per cent on taxable income above £32,011 and to 45 per cent on taxable income above £150,000 (2013/14 thresholds); in contrast, the Class 1 employee National Insurance contribution is 12 per cent on weekly earnings between £149 and £747 per week, and then falls to 2 per cent on earnings above that, although the employer contribution of 13.8 per cent continues on higher earnings (HMRC web site pages http://www.hmrc.gov.uk/rates/it.htm and http://www.hmrc.gov.uk/rates/nic.htm).

3   Original incomes are 'equivalised' using the modified OECD equivalisation scale. Because household members typically pool their incomes and living costs, all the income earned by members of a household is added up and is then notionally distributed among them, giving the household head one share for every half share awarded to

other adults, and a 0.3 share for each child. In this way, each individual ends up with his or her own notional income. I have discussed this procedure and the way it affects official estimates of 'child poverty' in Peter Saunders, 'Poverty of ambition', Policy Exchange Research Note, October 2009.

4   Abstracted from Office for National Statistics, 'The Effects of Taxes and Benefits on Household Income, 2010/2011', *Statistical Bulletin, 26 June 2012*, p.9

5   John Hills, *Inequality and the state*, 2004.

6   Originally published in John Hills with Karen Gardiner, *The Future of Welfare*, York: Joseph Rowntree Foundation, 1997, and later updated in John Hills, *Inequality and the state*, Oxford University Press, 2004. Their modeling was based on the tax and welfare system of the 1990s and this has changed significantly since (not least as a result of the huge increase in the use of tax credits). Jonathon Shaw at the Institute of Fiscal Studies is currently working on an updated model which is unlikely to be completed before 2014 (personal email correspondence, 16 May 2013).

7   Equivalised incomes take account of the number of people in a household who share that income. A worker with children thus has a lower equivalised income than another without, even if their actual earnings are the same.

8   From John Hills, *Inequality and the state*, Fig 8.6, p.196

9   The *Daily Telegraph* recently calculated lifetime income tax and National Insurance contributions (but not indirect tax payments) made to the welfare state and other government provisions by people on different average annual salaries, based on 2013 tax and spending. At an annual average income over 43 years of £35,000, someone ends up paying just over £360,000 in tax, of which £245,749 goes to pay for social security (£130,802), health (£65,581) and education (£49,366) (Robert Watts, 'Revealed: how much you pay towards benefits bill', *Daily Telegraph*, 8 June 2013).

10   It will be noted that, even in the highest decile, people on average appear to be deriving a small net lifetime benefit and are not self-financing all of their benefits. This seems odd given that we have already seen that, on average, people in this top decile are paying almost twice as much in tax than they are receiving in benefits. The explanation is that the figures for each decile are *averages*, and the average tax paid in these higher deciles is pulled down by the inclusion of individuals – like low-earning wives of highly-paid men – who live in high income households and are assumed to share in this high total household income but who themselves earn small incomes, meaning they pay relatively

little tax. As is common in analyses of income distribution, household members are credited with a share of total household income which is calculated by application of an equivalence scale, even if they earn little themselves. I am grateful to John Hills for clarifying this in personal email correspondence.

11   Hills, *Inequality and the state*, p.197, emphasis in original

12   My estimate is based on Ann Harding, *Lifetime Income Distribution and Redistribution*, Emerald Group, Bingley, 1993. Basing her analysis on Australian data for 1986 (and excluding the value of health and personal services received, and indirect taxes paid), Harding found: 'A significant proportion of income taxes paid during the lifetime are returned *to the same individuals* in the form of cash transfers during some other period of their lifecycle. Over the lifetime there is thus significant churning' (p.168, emphasis in original). I estimate this 'significant proportion' as in excess of 50 per cent in Peter Saunders, *The Government Giveth and the Government Taketh Away*, Sydney: Centre for Independent Studies, 2007, pp.28-31. See also: Jane Falkingham and Ann Harding, 'Poverty alleviation versus social insurance systems' NATSEM *Discussion Paper* No.12, 1996, University of Canberra; Rachel Lloyd, Ann Harding and Neil Warren, *Redistribution, the Welfare State and Lifetime Transitions*, NATSEM, Canberra, 2005.

13   These international comparisons are taken from A. Lans Bovenberg, Martin Hansen, Peter Sorensen, 'Individual savings accounts for social insurance', *International Tax Public Finance*, 2008, vol.15, 67-86; S. Foelster, 'Asset-based social insurance in Sweden', in S. Regan and W. Paxton (eds) *Asset-based welfare: International Experiences*, London: Institute for Public Policy Research, 2001.

14   Organisation for Economic Co-operation and Development (OECD), *Social Expenditure Database*; Peter Saunders and Andrew Baker, 'Introduction' to Tom Palmer, *After the Welfare State*, Sydney: Centre for Independent Studies, 2013

15   See for example, Frank Field, 'Bringing an end to something-for-nothing welfare', *The Sunday Times*, 3 March 2013

16   As Labour MP Frank Field notes: 'For the first time a sizeable part of the working class and lower middle class now have incomes that give them real choices' (Frank Field, *Welfare Titans*, London: Civitas, 2002, p.11).

17   The 'tragedy of the commons' refers to any situation where a resource (such as common land) is owned by everyone, so everybody has an incentive to use it to gain the maximum benefit for themselves (e.g. by overgrazing their animals on it) with little or no regard for the

long-term consequences. Even if one individual tries to be responsible, regulating their own use, others will take advantage by increasing theirs, so in the end, everyone goes for maximum exploitation and the resource itself swiftly collapses. See Garrett Hardin, 'The tragedy of the commons', *Science*, vol.162, 13 December 1968, pp.1243-1248. Obvious examples today include over-fishing the oceans, polluting the atmosphere with noxious emissions, and jamming the roads with private cars. To this list, we might also add the incentive to exploit 'free' welfare benefits and services.

18   This section is based on chapter 3 of Peter Saunders, *The Government Giveth and the Government Taketh Away.*

19   This represents a crucial difference between compulsory contributions into a personal fund and payment of taxes into a general government fund. In Australia, where employers make a nine per cent compulsory contribution to their employees' personal superannuation funds, it is sometimes argued that this contribution is tantamount to a tax, but this is misleading, for employees retain ownership of the money in their own funds.

20   Office for National Statistics estimates, reported in 'Barometer', *The Spectator*, 15 June 2013

21   The qualifying age for the state pension will rise to 66 in 2012 and to 67 by 2028. The link to future changes in life expectancy, announced in the 2012 budget, means that retirement age could reach 70 by 2047, and 73 by 2067. See 'New state pension age: when will you retire?', *This is Money*, 14 January 2013: http://www.thisismoney.co.uk/money/pensions/article-1679780/New-state-pension-age-retire.html

22   Joseph Stiglitz, believes this economic argument for replacing state social insurance with some system of personal accounts is compelling (*Economics of the public sector,* 3rd edn, W. W. Norton & Co, New York/London, 2000, chapter 14).

23   As Nicholas Barr points out: 'Whichever method is used, what matters is the level of output after I have retired. The point is fundamental... money is irrelevant unless the production is there for pensioners to buy.' (Nicholas Barr, *The Welfare State as Piggy Bank*, p.91)

24   'The threshold condition for self-respect is accepting responsibility for one's own life, for which the inescapable behavioral manifestation is earning one's own way in the world.' Charles Murray, *In Pursuit of Happiness and Good Government*, New York: Simon & Schuster, 1994, p.122

25   Charles Murray, *In Pursuit of Happiness and Good Government*, New York: Simon & Schuster, 1988, p.156. In a later book, Murray argues that the European welfare state model represents 'an ideal only for a

particular way of looking at life. It accepts that the purpose of life is to while away the time as pleasantly as possible, and the purpose of government to enable people to do so with as little effort as possible' (*In Our Hands,* AEI Press, 2006, p.84).

26   There is a parallel here with Marx's concept of alienation as a divorce from the essence of oneself as a human being (as well as from the objects of our own labour). Mauricio Rojas (*Beyond the welfare state,* Stockholm: Timbro, 2001, p.35) captures this in his discussion of tax-welfare churning: 'Only a very limited portion of what we pay in tax is redistributed between different social groups... The greater part really goes into a *whirligig which transforms our money into political power over ourselves*' (emphasis in original).

27   The architect of personal retirement accounts in Chile, Jose Pinera, notes that social security contributions were seen by Chilean workers as tax, but contributions to their personal pensions accounts are seen as private savings ('The success of Chile's privatized social security', *Cato Policy Report,* vol.18, No.4, 1995, p.10).

28   Osborne's comments were prompted by the case of Mike Philpott, an unemployed father of 14 children who was convicted in 2013 of killing six of them in a deliberate house fire. The court heard evidence of Philpott's chaotic and violent life on benefits. See BBC News, 'Mick Philpott case: George Osborne benefit comments spark row', 5 April 2013, http://www.bbc.co.uk/news/uk-politics-22025035

29   Bartholomew, *The Welfare State We're In*

30   Frank Field, *Neighbours From Hell* ,London: Politico's, 2003, p.33. He goes on: 'The idea that welfare should be received free of conditions is a very recent development. For most of the last 400 years the receipt of welfare has been dependent on fulfilling a series of conditions. Only since the 1960s did an opposing idea gain ground...[the] damaging belief that no matter how badly a person behaves, the right to welfare is inviolate' (pp. 95 and 98).

31   One problem with requiring claimants to pay a deductible is that it can make it difficult for genuine claimants to find the money to get the help they need. One way of getting around this problem is to link insurance to personal savings accounts, so claimants pay deductibles out of their own accounts. As we shall see below, this is a common feature of Medical Savings Accounts elsewhere in the world.

32   Eamonn Butler and Madsen Pirie, *The Fortune Account,* London: Adam Smith Institute, 1995

33   Meakin, *Abolish National Insurance,* p.32

34   Thomas Cawston, Andrew Haldenby, Patrick Nolan, *The End of*

Entitlement, London: Reform, October 2009, p.20

35   Patrick Nolan, Lauren Thorpe, Kimberley Trewhitt, *Entitlement Reform*

36   Matthew Oakley, 'Welfare reform must be based on the principle of something for something', *The Guardian*, 7 January 2013

37   Joseph Stiglitz and Jungyoll Yun, 'Integration of unemployment insurance with retirement insurance', *Journal of Public Economics*, vol.89, 2005, 2037-67

38   Provided the same people are not exposed to multiple risks at the same time, Stiglitz concludes that integration therefore minimises adverse incentive problems.

39   Joseph Stiglitz and Jungyoll Yun, 'Integration of unemployment insurance with retirement insurance' p.2041

40   Philip Johnston, 'The pensions revolution arriving by stealth', *Daily Telegraph*, 25 September 2012; Patrick Nolan, Lauren Thorpe, Kimberley Trewhitt, *Entitlement Reform*, Annex 2

41   Philip Johnston, 'The pensions revolution arriving by stealth'

42   Details on the NEST website http://www.nestpensions.org.uk/schemeweb/NestWeb/public/home/contents/homepage.html

43   Those earning less than £5,668 p.a. (2013/14) are 'entitled workers' who must be enrolled by employers if they make a request but who are not entitled to an employer's contribution. Those earning more than this, but less than £8,105, and those under 22 years of age, are 'eligible workers' who are only enrolled if they request it, but for whom employers must make a contribution.

44   Richard Thaler and Cass Sunstein, *Nudge: Improving Decisions About Health, Wealth and Happiness*, Yale University Press, 2008

45   A number of actuarial professionals have expressed concern that contributions have been set too low. See James Lloyd, *Personal accounts and pension reform after the credit crunch: A summary brief*, International Longevity Centre UK, 2009

46   'Nudge, nudge: A new scheme has potential drawbacks', *The Economist*, 6 October 2012

47   Stephen Kirchner, *Compulsory super at 20*

48   Stephen Kirchner, for example, thinks that the Australian compulsory superannuation system forces workers into an inferior form of saving which is more heavily taxed than alternatives like housing, and is less liquid than other alternatives like bank deposits or shares. As he notes: 'Mandatory savings programs... cannot possibly be optimal given the diversity of individual tastes, preferences, opportunities and life circumstances' (*Compulsory Super at 20*, p.17).

49 'The problem is that if you don't compel people to save, you end up with welfare again', Roger Douglas (former New Zealand Minister of Finance), interviewed by Susan Windybank in *Policy*, vol.19, No.2, Winter 2003, p.26

50 Sarah Levy, *Pensions in the National Accounts: A fuller picture of the UK's funded and unfunded pension obligations*, Pensions Analysis Unit, Office for National Statistics, 27 April 2012

51 Nor, for that matter, are other unfunded government liabilities (such as payments owing on PFI investments or the cost of decommissioning nuclear power stations) included in national debt calculations. These amount to another £500 billion. See Emma Boon, 'Why we should include PFI in the national debt', http://www.taxpayersalliance.com/campaign/2011/08/include-pfi-national-debt.html

52 David Kingman, *Can the UK Afford to Pay for Pensions?*, Intergenerational Foundation, March 2013, p.5

53 Kingman, *Can the UK Afford to Pay for Pensions?*

54 Whiteford and Standing, *Targeting, adequacy and incentives*, pp.9-10

55 Barbara Kritzer, 'Individual accounts in other countries', *Social Security Bulletin*, vol.66, no.1, 2005

56 Bob Davis and Matt Moffett, 'From nations that have tried similar pensions, some lessons', *Wall Street Journal*, 3 February 2005; Barr, *The welfare state as piggy bank*, 138-9

57 See D. McCarthy, Mitchell, O and J. Piggott, *Asset Rich and Cash Poor: Retirement provision and housing policy in Singapore*, Pension Research Council Working Paper, Wharton School, University of Pennsylvania, 2001

58 Singapore Provident Fund website, http://mycpf.cpf.gov.sg/CPF/About-Us/CPF-Stats/CPF_Stats2012q4.htm

59 Luke Buckmaster, 'Medical Savings Accounts: a possible health reform for Australia?', Parliamentary Library *Research Note*, 23 March 2006, Parliament of Australia

60 Mukul Asher, 'The Singapore model' in Eamonn Butler, Mukul Ashaer and Karl Borden, *Singapore versus Chile*, Adam Smith Institute, 1996

61 Mukul Asher, 'The Singapore model'

62 Singapore Central Provident Fund Board, http://mycpf.cpf.gov.sg/Employers/Gen-Info/cpf-Contri/ContriRa.htm

63 Singapore Provident Fund website http://mycpf.cpf.gov.sg/CPF/About-Us/Intro/Intro.htm

64 Eamonn Butler and Madsen Pirie, *The fortune account*. As we saw in Part I, Britain's 1909 pension scheme was funded out of taxation, and it

was not until the 1930s that it was put on a contributory basis.

65   Karl Bordern, 'How Chile broke the pensions chain letter'; L Jacabo Rodriguez, 'Chile's private pension system at 18', Washington: Cato Institute, *Social Security Paper* No.17, July 1999

66   Peter Ferrara, 'A personal account option for social security', *Forbes*, 31 March 2011. The state guarantees to make up any shortfall in pension to 85 per cent of the minimum wage.

67   Gonzalo Reyes Hartley, Jan van Ours, Milan Vodopivec, 'Incentive effects of unemployment savings accounts: Evidence from Chile', *Discussion Paper* No 4681, January 2010, Forschungsinstitut zur Zukunft der Arbeit (IZA), Bonn. Individual accounts and the Solidarity Fund are only available to claimants who have made at least 12 months of contributions. The Solidarity Fund can only be accessed by those who are unemployed through no fault of their own, and it can only be claimed for five months, with payments declining each month from 50 per cent of former salary in month one to 30 per cent in month five. No more than two claims on the Solidarity Fund can be made in any five year period.

68   A *South China Morning Post* survey published on 25 August 2000 found that only 44 per cent of respondents believed that their funds were sufficient to cover their retirement needs.

69   It is estimated that in 1998 about 38 per cent of workers – mostly self-employed or in the informal sector – were outside the scheme (Sebastian Edwards and Alejandra Cox Edwards, 'Social security privatization reform and labor markets: The case of Chile', *Economic Development and Cultural Change*, vol.50, April 2002, 465-89

70   Jose Pinera, 'The success of Chile's privatised social security'

71   Sebastian Edwards and Alejandra Edwards, 'Social security privatization reform and labor markets', National Bureau of Economic Research, *Working Paper* No.8924, 2002, p.468. See also: E. Huber, 'Options for social policy in Latin America' in G. Esping-Andersen (ed.), *Welfare States in Transition*, London: Sage, 1996; James Payne, 'How America drifted from welfare to entitlement', *The American Enterprise*, March 2005, vol.16, 26-33; Larry Rohter, 'Chile's retirees find shortfall in private plan' *New York Times* 27 January 2005

72   Insurance experts meeting in London in 2009 broadly opposed the use of workplace pension accounts for other purposes on the grounds that 'the conditions under which individuals can withdraw pension saving will become increasingly relaxed, ultimately undermining pension saving'. James Lloyd, *Personal Accounts and Pension Reform After the Credit Crunch: A summary brief*, International Longevity Centre UK, 2009, p.5

73   A. Lans Bovenberg, Martin Hansen, Peter Sorensen, 'Efficient

redistribution of lifetime income through welfare accounts', *Fiscal Studies*, vol.33, 2012, 1-37. The authors show (p.24) that if all these benefits, as well as the retirement pension, were transferred from the welfare system to personal accounts, the impact on the lifetime distribution of income in Denmark would be tiny (an increase in the Gini coefficient from 0.127 to 0.133).

74 A. Lans Bovenberg, Martin Hansen, Peter Sorensen, 'Individual savings accounts for social insurance', p.84

75 In May 2013, 727,155 people (48.7 per cent of all JSA claimants) were unemployed for more than six months. Office for National Statistics, *Official Labour Market Statistics*, http://www.nomisweb.co.uk/articles/739.aspx

76 Debra Leaker, 'Sickness absence from work in the UK', *Economic and Labour Market Review*, vol.2, Nov 2008, 18-22. The difference between public and private sector workers is interesting in itself.

77 Parental leave should not be confused with maternity and paternity leave – time off work immediately preceding and after a child is born. Women currently have a right to 39 weeks of paid maternity leave, and men can claim one or two weeks of paid paternity leave (they may also share some of the maternity leave entitlement of the mother). The cost in both cases is borne by the employer.

78 'Individual accounts may improve the sustainability of the welfare state by inducing people not to take up social benefits unless they really need them.' A. Lans Bovenberg, Martin Hansen, Peter Sorensen, 'Efficient redistribution of lifetime income through welfare accounts', p.36

79 Gonzalo Reyes Hartley, Jan van Ours, Milan Vodopivec, 'Incentive effects of unemployment savings accounts: Evidence from Chile', pp.4 & 14

80 Allowing people to borrow to tide them over short periods of hardship (rather than giving them state benefits) would maintain a strong incentive to return to employment, in order to limit their debt. Stiglitz suggests that use of loans avoids the severe adverse incentive effects associated with state benefits or insurance, because people are still ultimately drawing on their own money. Joseph Stiglitz and Jungyoll Yun, 'Integration of unemployment insurance with retirement insurance'

81 Stefan Folster, 'Social insurance based on personal savings accounts', Stockholm: Industrial Institute for Economic and Social Research, *Working Paper* No.454, 1996, p.4

82 Gonzalo Reyes Hartley, Jan van Ours, Milan Vodopivec, 'Incentive effects of unemployment savings accounts: Evidence from Chile', p.6

83 See, for example, Economics Focus, 'Dolling up the dole', *The*

Economist, 23 September 2006, p.80

84   Gonzalo Reyes Hartley, Jan van Ours, Milan Vodopivec, 'Incentive effects of unemployment savings accounts: Evidence from Chile', p.6

85   Judgement of someone's incapacity is made at a Personal Capability Assessment, although those presenting evidence of severe disability or illness may not have to attend for assessment.

86   Shorter periods of impairment can, of course, be covered by savings, loans or insurance, and private disability insurance has apparently been introduced successfully in a number of countries including the Netherlands, Finland, Switzerland and Canada (Thomas Cawston, Andrew Haldenby, Patrick Nolan, *The end of entitlement*, p.17).

87   This is something Labour MP Frank Field has advocated for some time (e.g. Frank Field and Patrick White, *Welfare Isn't Working*, London: Reform, May 2007), and which Labour leader Ed Miliband has also recently begun to endorse (Roland Watson, 'I can be tough on welfare benefits too, insists Miliband', *The Times*, 6 June 2013). Labour's Liam Byrne also recently proposed that unemployed people with many years of NICs should qualify for a higher rate of JSA: 'Why Conservative benefit cuts won't get Britain working', *The Observer*, 6 April 2013; James Kirkup, 'Higher benefits for older unemployed, says Labour', *Daily Telegraph*, 24 June 2013.

88   It is probably not a viable policy even if we stay with the existing system. As we saw when discussing Beveridge's reforms in Part I, non-contributory benefits have to be set at a level sufficient to enable claimants to maintain an adequate, basic standard of living, which means that giving more to those with a strong contributions record entails raising the value of contributory benefits. This is almost certainly unaffordable given the problem of the government deficit, and it is also arguably undesirable, for higher benefits reduce people's incentive to organize additional insurance for themselves as well as weakening the motivation to find another job (which is why Beveridge did not like the idea).

89   Richard Crisp and Del Roy Fletcher, 'A comparative review of workfare programmes in the United States, Canada and Australia', DWP, *Research Report* No.533, 2008; Paul Gregg, *Realising Potential*, HMSO, 2008, p.88.

90   Julia Griggs and Martin Evans, *Sanctions within conditional benefit systems*, Joseph Rowntree Foundation, 2010, p.20

91   Robert Goodin, 'False principles of welfare reform', *Australian Journal of Social Issues*, vol. 36, 2001, 189-206

92   Nicholas Boys-Smith, *Reforming welfare*, p.23

93   Department of Employment & Workplace Relations, *Work for the*

Dole: A Net Impact Study Commonwealth of Australia, Canberra, 2000, p.12

94   Charles Murray draws a parallel with vehicle insurance: 'Taking care of your health-care needs should be like keeping your car on the road. You pay for the ordinary upkeep with cash and use insurance to protect against expensive accidents.' *In Our Hands*, p.43

95   Michael Cannon, 'Answering the critics of health accounts', *Brief Analysis* No.454, Washington D.C.: National Center for Policy Analysis, September 2003

96   Thomas Massaro and Yu-Niong Wong, 'Positive experience with Medical Savings Accounts in Singapore', *Health Affairs*, Summer 1995, 267-72; Luke Buckmaster, 'Medical Savings Accounts: a possible health reform option for Australia?' Parliament of Australia *Research Note*, 23 March 2006, Parliamentary Library, Canberra.

97   The obvious concern is that people might put their health at risk by trying to cut their treatment costs, but studies suggest this does not happen. In a US randomised trial, people using heavily-subsidised health plans achieved no better health outcomes than a group which had to meet more of its costs from their own pockets, and in South Africa, researchers found no evidence of MSA patients foregoing necessary treatment in an attempt to protect their savings. Cannon, 'Answering the critics of health accounts'

98   Emma Simon, 'How to cope with long-term care costs', *Daily Telegraph*, 13 June 2013

99   'There will need to be a clearer recognition of the need for families to consider options like drawing down the equity built up in their homes', Patrick Nolan, Lauren Thorpe, Kimberley Trewhitt, *Entitlement Reform*, p.9. The authors say that £907bn is tied up in houses owned by pensioners.

100   Emma Simon, 'How to cope with long-term care costs'

101   A means test will reduce the burden on those with assets below £123,000, but this includes the family home, so many home-owners will still have to sell, despite government claims to the contrary. As we saw earlier, some commentators, such as the Reform think-tank, believe individuals should in principle be expected to use the capital in their homes to help fund their own welfare requirements.

102   David Brindle, 'Labour risks another "death tax" row with social care blueprint', *The Guardian*, 24 January 2013

103   To safeguard against familiar 'market failure' problems (e.g. to ensure that everyone can find affordable insurance), government would probably have to impose certain 'community rating' and 'guaranteed

issue' conditions on insurers (e.g. companies issuing policies would be required to treat the entire population as a single risk-pool and would have to accept anyone who applies for a policy – the so-called 'taxi-rank' principle). See Nicholas Barr, *The Welfare State as Piggy Bank*, p.65 for a discussion of strategies for overcoming market failure in private insurance.

Conclusion: Making the Transition

1   Stuart Adam and Glen Loutzenhiser, *Integrating income tax and national insurance*

2   The IFS points out that, even if benefits are universal, some way is still needed to prevent newcomers to Britain from accessing benefits they haven't paid for.

3   Stuart Adam and Glen Loutzenhiser, p.55

4   Vuk Vukovic, 'Unburdening enterprise', Adam Smith Institute, *Briefing Paper* 2012

5   We saw in Part I that men often spend more years in the labour force than women, and therefore build up stronger state pension entitlements. It is for this reason that women who raise young children at home are now deemed to have made NI payments, even though they have actually paid nothing at all. If we move to a residency qualification, men and women alike will get the state pension, irrespective of their work histories.

6   One of the many advantages of abolishing National Insurance and switching to a simple residency qualification for the state pension is that the special categories of people 'deemed' by the government to have made NICs, even when they have made no financial contribution at all, can be consigned to history. This sort of ad hoc special treatment is in principle undesirable, for it allows politicians to favour some sections of the population over others, it encourages special pleading by sectional interest groups, and it weakens the principle of the Rule of Law.

7   Figures from Patrick Nolan, 'Scrap the winter fuel allowance', *Prospect* magazine blog, 1 May 2013, http://www.prospectmagazine.co.uk/blog/winter-fuel-allowance-pensoners-bus-pass/#.Udmo6PmTiSo

8   Point 5, below, discusses how entitlements built up under the old system should be honoured in the transition to a new, tax-funded, means-tested state pension system.

9   By 2047, 76.4 per cent of Australian retirees are expected to qualify for some state pension, 36 per cent getting a full pension. Currently, 80 per cent get something, and 55 per cent get the full pension. Kirchner, *Compulsory Super at 20*, pp.16-17

10 'Postal workers say Royal Mail sell off would be a disaster', BBC News website, 22 April 2012, http://www.bbc.co.uk/news/business-17807772

11 James Barty and Emily Redding, *Privatising the banks*, London: Policy Exchange, 2013

12 Not only would 40 million individual shareholders create an unwieldy shareholder base for these companies, but giving people something for nothing (by giving shares to people who pay no taxes) is precisely the wrong message for government to be sending out. On the original proposal, see Patrick Wintour, 'Nick Clegg calls for public to get shares in bailed-out banks', *The Guardian*, 23 June 2011

13 Barty and Redding suggest some bank shares should be sold to the financial institutions, to raise about £14bn, and the rest should be distributed to any taxpayers (defined as anyone with a NI number) who apply for them on a deferred payment basis, the original sale price being paid only when they sell the shares. Some variant of this proposal could be adapted to the proposal outlined here. For example, eligibility could be limited to taxpayers with workplace pension funds, and the requirement could be set that the shares be kept in these funds until sold, with dividends and eventual capital gains sheltered from tax.

14 In the two-year period of grace between the scrapping of NICs and the ending of contributory unemployment benefit, someone on a wage of £26,500 (the average wage in 2012 according to the Office for National Statistics, *Annual Survey of Hours and Earnings*, 22 November 2012) would accumulate £5,830 in their workplace savings fund (assuming an 11 per cent total contribution). If they were out of work for the full six months (after which they would have to apply for benefits), they could pay themselves the Jobseeker's Allowance basic rate for somebody aged 25 or over of £71.70 p.w. (see DWP, *Benefit and pension rates*, April 2013, http://www.dwp.gov.uk/docs/dwp035.pdf), which amounts to £1,864.20, or 32 per cent of their savings.